Simple
QUILTS
FOR THE MODERN HOME

by Stephanie Soebbing

Simple Quilts for the Modern Home
by Stephanie Soebbing

Landauer Publishing (www.landauerpub.com) is an imprint of
Fox Chapel Publishing Company, Inc.

Copyright © 2019 by Stephanie Soebbing and
Fox Chapel Publishing Company, Inc.
903 Square Street, Mount Joy, PA 17552.

Project Team:
Vice President-Content: Christopher Reggio
Editors: Laurel Albright/Sue Voegtlin
Copy Editor: Katie Ocasio
Designer: Laurel Albright
Photographer: Sue Voegtlin; Stephanie Soebbing

ISBN: 978-1-947163-03-4

The Cataloging-in-Publication Data is on file with the
Library of Congress.

We are always looking for talented authors.
To submit an idea, please send a brief inquiry to
acquisitions@foxchapelpublishing.com.

Printed in Singapore

21 20 19   2 4 6 8 10 9 7 5 3 1

TABLE OF CONTENTS

Introduction

My quilting journey started out of a need to set aside my hectic work schedule and focus on some creative time that I desperately needed. At first I struggled with quilting. Every stitch, seam, and set of instructions caused frustration and I needed help. Then I discovered my local quilting guild, Mississippi Valley Quilters Guild in the Quad Cities in Illinois and Iowa. It was a large guild with about 300 members that regularly brought in regional and national instructors. I finally found a resource to help me improve. I took at least one class every month on every technique I could find so I could learn as much as possible.

By 2011, I was the one teaching the classes. While the guild I loved had taught me so much, most of the quilts at Show and Tell were traditional. I appreciated the craftsmanship and had made more than a few quilts that fit in just fine. But I knew that traditional fabrics, colors, and patterns just didn't resonate with me.

When nearly 30 people signed up for a class to make a Lone Star quilt, nearly everyone showed up with fabrics you'd expect to find in a classic quilt pattern—light backgrounds, reproduction fabric, or repetitive small patterned fabric. I came with a black background and bright vibrant solids forming a rainbow in the center of the diamond. I chose fabrics that made me happy, not ones that matched my bedroom decor.

I started designing my own patterns, using the brightest colors I could find at my local quilt shops. Bright, fun, funky prints worked best with my tastes and looked appropriate in a modern, contemporary home.

Through my blog, *QuiltAddictsAnonymous*, I was invited to interview Kaffe Fassett in person at the opening of an exhibit of his quilts. The trip completely transformed my thoughts on quilt design. When I arrived and saw the bright colors, no-neutral quilts, and that 12-inch blocks are nice, but not necessary.

I read Kaffe's autobiography to prep for the interview. I only had a few minutes with him, and as a former journalist I wanted to be prepared. I realized no matter what Kaffe created—paintings, knitwear, fabric, quilts— everything he did was a reflection of his true self. He created what his soul needed and success followed.

The designs for this book started coming to me in the middle of the night on the way home from the exhibit. By the time we arrived home half of the designs were sketched out. That's how the seeds for *Simple Quilts for the Modern Home* were planted.

Staying true to myself and my mission to make quilting easy and accessible to everyone, I have created 12 quilts that are simple to piece. Some look more complicated than others, but once you break them down, any of these quilts can be made by a confident beginner or an advanced quilter looking for a fast project.

Happy Quilting,
Stephanie Soebbing

Let's Get Started!

I use all my pattern design go-tos to make the quilting process as simple and streamlined as possible – strip piecing, making triangles from squares, and fusible appliqué – so you can create these quilts and convince your friends you spent hours and hours piecing the perfect quilt top. It'll be our little secret . . . and everyone else who has bought the book will know, but they'll keep quiet too. We'll also cover fabric selection and quilting decisions in each pattern, because those components can make or break a design. Let's get started!

Principles of Modern Design

There is no one way to define modern quilting. What is modern to one quilter leans toward traditional to another. Still, there are a few design elements that are consistent across manyxmodern quilt designs: alternative grid, expansive negative space, embracing minimalism, and modernizing traditional blocks.

Alternative Grid

Simply put, alternative grid means you break the traditional grid structure of a quilt design where you make a specific number of blocks and sew them together in rows with or without sashing and a border. It can be as simple as changing the focus from the center of the quilt to a corner or side of the quilt, like Houndstooth or Ripples. By shifting the focus from the traditional center, the quilt becomes more modern in design and appearance.

Houndstooth, page 28

Ripples, page 34

You also could do away with the block structure all together like in Bricks and Pavers. This quilt is still connected in rows but there is no block. The visual interest is created by fabric choice and placement rather than a complicated block design.

Bricks and Pavers, page 42

Expansive Negative Space

Many modern quilts make use of large areas of negative space. I made use of this technique in many of the quilts, but my favorite is Diamond. This helps emphasize the parts of the quilt that are meant to shine through intricate piecing, design or fabric selection, and provides a fabulous canvas for quilting.

Embracing Minimalism

Ombré and Stripes are both examples of minimalist quilts. Gradually fading colors in Ombré and bold modern fabrics in Stripes make them pop. Color selection, fabric choice, and simple piecing all contribute to the minimal look of a quilt.

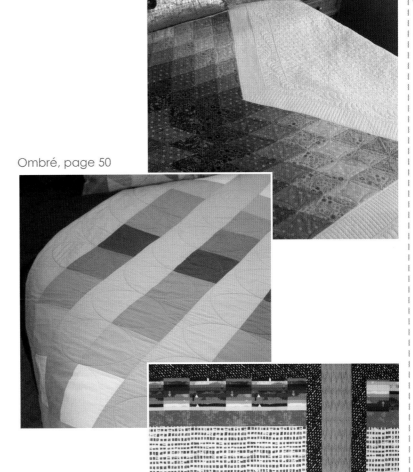

Diamond, page 74

Ombré, page 50

Stripes, page 46

Modernizing Traditional Blocks

Flying Geese is one of the most traditional and well-known blocks in quilting. In Going North I modernized this design by creating the flying wgeese from strip-pieced half-square triangles. I arranged them in an alternate grid setting with expansive negative space on either side. Think about your favorite quilt block and how you can give it a makeover so it will fit in to today's trendiest home.

Going North, page 24

Essential Tools

If you are just starting out, there are "must have" tools and then there are the additional tools that will make your projects come together faster and easier. Here are some of the essentials you want to consider before getting started, what they do and why you might want to try them.

Sewing Machine

This may seem like a no-brainer but a machine is the first and most important tool you will need to learn how to quilt. You don't need anything fancy to start. As long as it will sew a straight stitch and it's clean, you'll be fine.

If you do purchase a new machine, I recommend buying one from a local store where you can learn how to use it and they will service it for you.

Quarter-Inch Presser Foot

Every quilt pattern I've ever read is written for a ¼" (0.64cm) seam allowance. The easiest way to maintain a consistent seam is to use a ¼" (0.64cm) presser foot. Some feet maintain this measurement when the needle is centered and the seam is sewn along the outer edge of the foot. Other types have a small metal guide to move your fabric along when you are sewing a seam. Machines might come with a dedicated ¼" (0.64cm) foot or there are after-market feet available.

Walking Foot

A walking foot is used any time you are moving three or more layers through your sewing machine. The walking foot is special because it has small ridges, or "feed dogs," on top of the foot that move in tandem with the feed dogs under the throat plate of your machine. Layers are moved through the machine at the same rate, preventing bunching or puckers.

Thread

Choosing a good thread helps avoid headaches as you sew. It can help avoid lint build-up, extending the time you can go between cleanings. When you move from piecing to quilting, thread choice plays a powerful role in the finished look of the quilt.

For piecing and quilting I use Aurifil™ 50wt thread. I like to piece with white thread no matter what color of fabric I'm working with and I use all colors to quilt with.

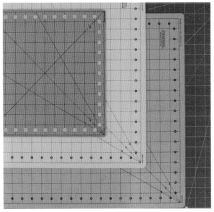

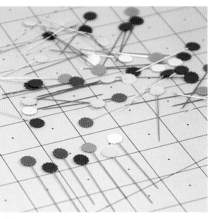

Rotary Cutters

To the untrained eye, a rotary cutter looks and works like a pizza cutter. A rotary cutter allows you to cut fabric quickly, easily, and accurately with the aid of an acrylic ruler or template. There are many options on the market but they all do the same thing. The blades are very sharp and they can cut quickly and unexpectedly if you aren't careful with them. Always make sure your blade is in the safety setting when you aren't using it.

Cutting Mats

I suggest you buy no smaller than an 18" x 24" (45.72 x 60.96cm) self-healing cutting mat. You'll be able to cut strips across the width of fabric and that is required for nearly every pattern in this book. Mats are gridded to assist you in cutting, but it's important to make sure 1" (2.54cm) squares of the grid are accurate.

Pins

You need something to hold your fabric together as you sew, and pins are that something! I prefer flower-head pins because they slide easily into quilting fabric, they're easy to grab on to, and they're cute! Try to find long, thin pins for easier handling.

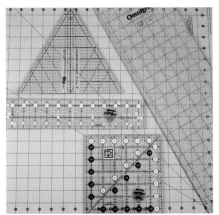

Quilting Rulers

Acrylic quilting rulers come in all shapes and sizes but the 6" x 24" (15.24 x 60.96cm) ruler is one of the most versatile. They span the width of folded fabric and can be used to cut strips, squares, and even triangles. Try to find one with 30°, 45°, and 60° lines on it so you can also use it to trim triangle blocks. For smaller cuts, try a 6½" (16.51cm) square or a 2" (5.08cm) to 4" x 12" (10.16cm x 30.48cm) rectangular ruler for cutting, trimming, and squaring up pieces.

Batting

This is the warm layer that goes in between the quilt top and backing fabric. It provides warmth and creates texture to the top when quilted. I prefer Quilters Dream® batting and alternate between 100% cotton and 80/20 cotton/poly blend. Natural fibers help the cotton quilting fabric stick to the batting, making it easier to keep the fabric from bunching, especially if you are quilting on your home machine.

One other consideration for batting is color. It comes in natural, white, and black. I use white batting if there are white or gray neutrals in my quilt. I like the look of bleached white batting behind these colors. When I am working with a very dark or black background, I opt for black polyester batting. Occasionally bits of batting will get pushed through the quilting stitches and if you use black batting, you will never see it.

Quilting Fabric

When you start quilting, buy the best fabric you can afford. It will be well worth it in the end. Quilt shop quality cotton is always worth the money because the thread count is higher, the fabric holds its shape, and it's usually softer.

To choose your fabric, start by finding a focal print that you love. Then pick supporting prints that complement the focal fabric. One great way to find coordinating colors is to choose prints from one fabric line. Most lines have 12 to 24 coordinating prints so you can't go wrong.

When I'm planning a scrappy quilt, I often choose two colors and raid my stash for fabrics that work in that theme. (Of course, if you're just starting to quilt, you may not have this option.) I recommend buying a neutral to tie them all together. Neutral doesn't mean white or tan. One of the quilts in this book uses lime green as a neutral.

Perfect Piecing

There are two skills you need to master to create perfect piecing. Accurate cutting is the first, followed by sewing an accurate ¼" (0.64cm) seam. Quilting fabric comes from the store folded in half with selvages touching. The selvage is the edge on each side of the fabric that prevents it from unraveling. Leave your fabric folded when you start. The edge that was cut from the bolt will need to be straightened. Starting with a straight fabric edge will guarantee accurate cuts.

Straightening the Fabric

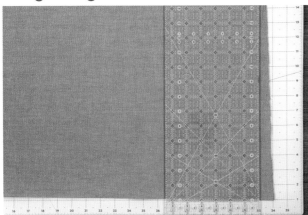

1. Lay the fabric on a cutting mat with cut side toward the right side of the mat. Smooth out any wrinkles. With the fold at the bottom of the mat, place a 6" x 24" (15.24 x 60.96cm) ruler on the fabric so that it spans the entire width of fabric. Align the ruler so the 1" (2.54cm) line is even with the fold of the fabric. Extend the fabric beyond the ruler's edge, just enough to straighten the fabric.

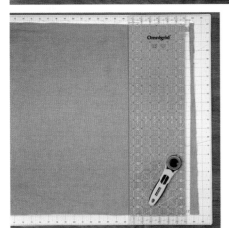

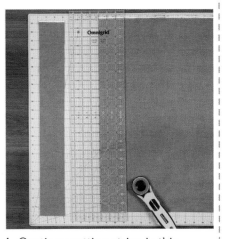

2. Hold the ruler down firmly with the palm of your hand and use a rotary cutter to cut along the ruler's edge.

3. Flip fabric to the left side of cutting mat and realign the ruler on the 1" (2.54cm) line. For example, we're cutting a 3" (7.62cm) strip. Align the 3" (7.62cm) line of the ruler along the straightened edge of the fabric. Repeat step 2 and cut the strip.

4. Continue cutting strips in this manner. As long as the 1" (2.54cm) line of ruler is on the fabric fold and the line of the required strip width aligns along the edge of the fabric, you will have straight, accurate strips. If you are cutting a lot of strips, it's a good idea to occasionally check the fabric edge to make sure it's still straight. Check by repeating step one.

Cutting Diamonds

I used the Clearview Triangle™ for all the 60° triangles and diamond cuts in this book. Some rulers have blunt tips but the Clearview has three points intact. Yardage requirements are based on the use of this ruler so it's important to use one with three sharp points for your project. The following step-by-step is for cutting diamonds for the Argyle quilt, page 64 and Diamond quilt, page 74. Regardless of the strip size, the instructions for lining up the ruler are the same for any size diamond you want to cut. Refer to specific instructions for strip size.

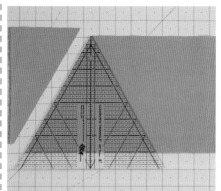 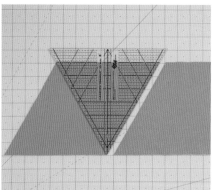 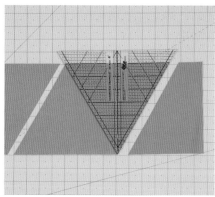

1. On a 7" (17.78cm) x WOF strip, line up the Clearview Triangle ruler on the 7" (17.78cm) line of the ruler. The tip and bottom of ruler should align with the top and bottom of the strip as shown. Cut off the corner and discard.

2. Flip the ruler and realign with the 7" (17.78cm) line on top of the strip and the point aligned with corner of fabric as shown. Cut along the right side of the ruler to create a diamond.

3. There is no need to flip the ruler for cuts. Move the ruler along the fabric strip, realigning as you cut.

Cutting Triangles

This step-by-step demonstrates how to cut triangles for the Ombré Star (page 68) and On the 60 (page 60) quilts. The instructions are the same for any size triangle you want to cut.

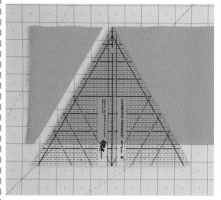 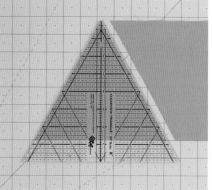 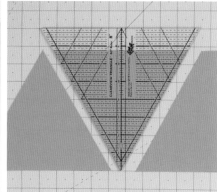

1. On a 6¾" (17.15cm) x WOF strip, line up the 60° triangle ruler on the 6¾" (17.15cm) line ¼" away from the edge, as shown. Cut off the corner and reserve the half triangles.

2. With the ruler in place, cut along the right side of the ruler to create a triangle.

3. Flip ruler back and forth, realigning and cutting triangles as you move across the strip of fabric.

Cutting 90° Triangles

This step-by-step demonstrates how to cut triangles for the Going North (page 24) and Houndstooth (page 38) quilts. The instructions are the same for any size triangle you want to cut.

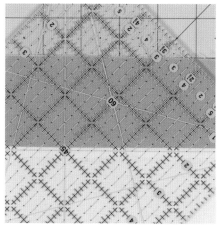
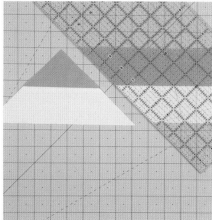
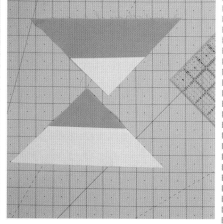

1. Align the 45° line of a ruler on the seam line between the strips. Cut along the left side of the ruler to create a right angle-triangle. Discard this strip.

2. Align the ruler so the edge is even with the tip of the strip set, and the 45° line is on the seam line. Cut to make a 90° triangle.

3. Reposition the ruler so the edge is even with the tip of the strip set and the 45° line is on the seam line. Cut along the right side of the ruler to make another 90° triangle.

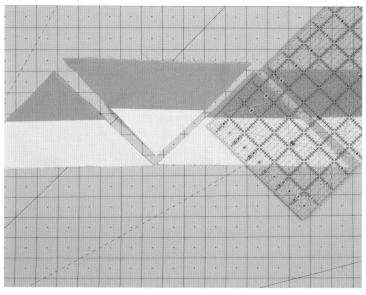

4. Continue repositioning the ruler, always keeping the 45° line of the ruler on the seam line. You can make eight 90° triangles from a width of fabric strip set.

Piecing

The other skill to perfect piecing is sewing an accurate ¼" (0.64cm) seam. Not all ¼" (0.64cm) feet are identical, since manufacturers make them specifically for their sewing machines. If your machine comes with one, that's great. If not, you'll still be able to sew a perfect seam without one.

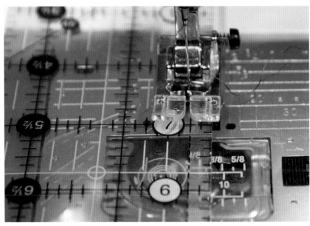

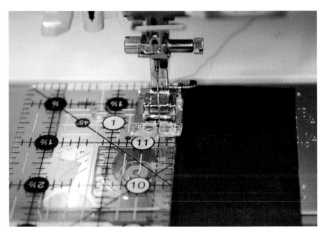

1. With the needle aligned on the quarter inch line of a ruler, you can see that this foot won't sew a ¼" (0.64cm) seam.

2. Take a piece of tape and lay it against the edge of the ruler, pressing the tape down on the throat of your machine. Use the edge of the tape as your ¼" (0.64cm) guide.

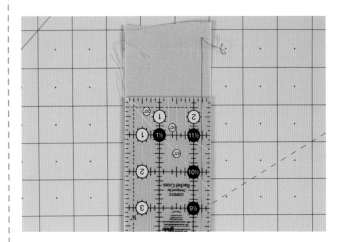

3. However you choose to sew your seam, it's a good idea to check it for accuracy. An extra ⅛" (0.32cm) may not seem like a lot, but those eighths can add up quickly and you may end up with pieces not fitting together.

Pro Tip:
Some patterns tell you to sew a scant ¼" (0.64cm) seam, for instance, when making half-square triangles. When a half-square triangle is folded open at the seam, it actually takes up a couple threads. By sewing a couple threads short of the ¼" (0.64cm), you will maintain the correct size of your half-square triangle.

Strip Piecing

Strip piecing is a great way to speed up your quilting. Layer two pieces right sides together, sew along the long side. Continue adding pieces in this manner until you have a set of multiple strips.

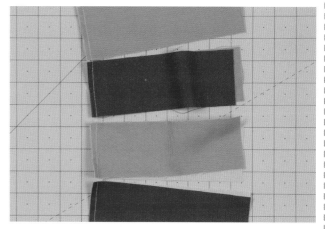

Half-Square Triangles

There are many ways to sew half-square triangles but my favorite way is to make them from squares. I can get two-for-one triangles and it's easier than sewing individual triangles on the bias since it avoids fabric stretch.

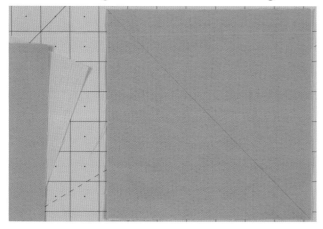

1. Draw a diagonal line from corner to corner on the wrong side of a square. Layer right sides together with a second square.

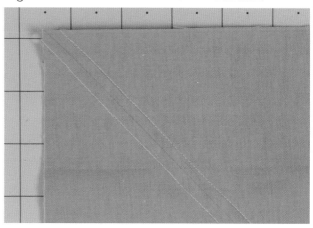

2. Sew a scant ¼" (0.64cm) seam on either side of the drawn line.

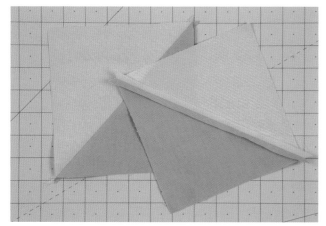

3. Cut on the drawn line, open, and press seams.

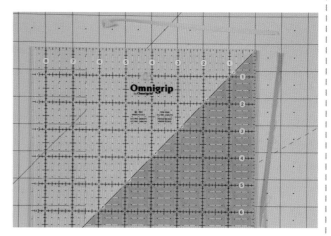

4. Square up the half-square triangles to the measurement in the project.

Equilateral Triangles

All equilateral triangles and diamonds in this book are cut from the Clearview Triangle ruler. I find the 8" (20.32cm) version most versatile. With three sharp points, I can line up my pieces quickly, pin, and sew. The fabric ears are called "dog ears" and they become a good reference as you align the pieces.

Triangles and diamonds are sewn in diagonal rows, which takes away the need to sew dreaded Y-seams. Since the pieces are cut on the bias, the seams can be stretchy. It's important to pin pieces together and not pull, push, or stretch the fabric as it goes through your machine. I like to use a double pinning method on all my 60° quilts to ensure the points come together perfectly.

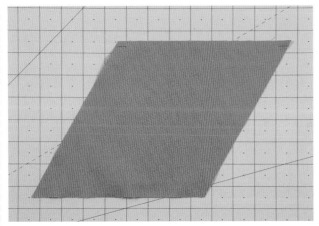

1. Align the ¼" (0.64cm) mark of a ruler along the edge of the diamond shape. With a pencil, draw a small line at both points to mark the seam line.

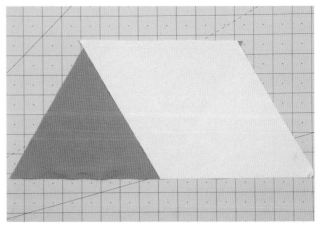

2. Layer a second diamond, right sides together. Align the ¼" (0.64cm) marks with edge of the second piece. The dog ears should extend a ¼" (0.64cm) beyond the edge of the fabric as shown.

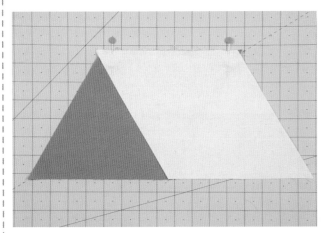

3. Pin the pieces at each point of the diamond and sew with a ¼" (0.64cm) seam. The seam should intersect in the valleys formed by the offset of the dog ears.

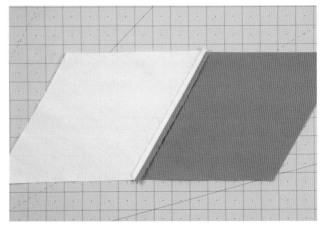

4. I always press open the seams of triangles and diamonds to make my quilt top lay flat.

Large Background Triangles

The Diamond quilt, on page 74, uses large background triangles to surround the blocks. You will need a 6" x 24" (16.24 x 60.96cm) ruler with 30° and 60° lines to cut the triangles.

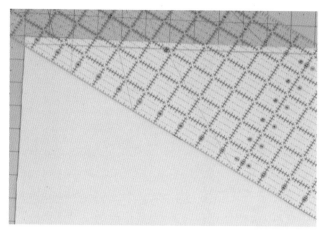

1. Select a strip and cut off the selvage to square up the fabric. Draw a ¼" (0.64cm) line along this edge. Open the strip, and align the 30° line of the ruler with the drawn line as shown.

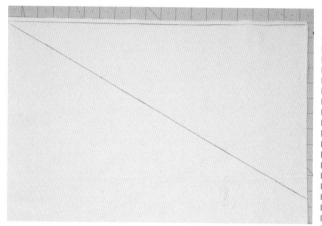

2. Draw a line along the edge of the ruler. Move the ruler along the drawn line to extend it to the edge of the fabric, to make one half of an equilateral triangle.

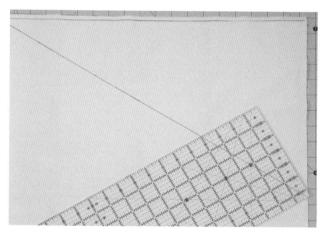

3. Align the 60° line of the ruler on the drawn line as shown. Draw along the ruler edge to make a 60° equilateral triangle.

4. Draw a line ¼" (0.64cm) away from the line you just drew. Cut on the lines of the equilateral triangle to make one large and two half-square equilateral triangles.

Large Background Triangles (continued)

The Ombré Star quilt, on page 68, uses large background triangles to surround the blocks. You will need a 6" x 24" (16.24 x 60.96cm) ruler with 30° and 60° lines to cut the triangles.

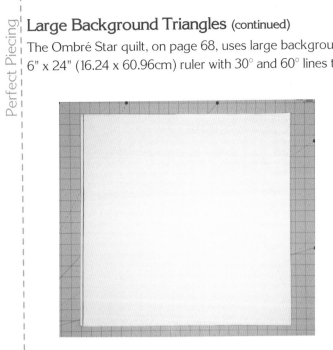

1. Select a strip and cut off the selvage to square up the fabric. Draw a ¼" (0.64cm) line along this edge.

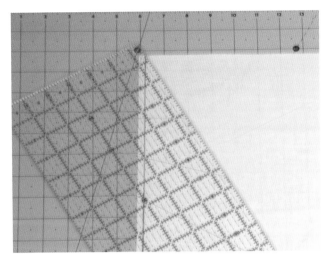

2. Open the strip and align the 30° line of the ruler on the drawn line as shown. Draw a line to create one half-equilateral triangle.

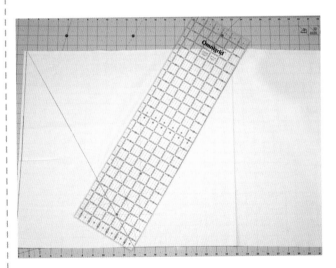

3. Align the 60° line of the ruler on the edge of the fabric as shown. Draw along the ruler edge to make a 60° equilateral triangle.

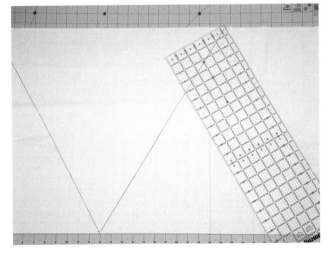

4. Realign the ruler to make a second equilateral triangle. Move the ruler along the drawn line to extend it to the edge of the fabric.

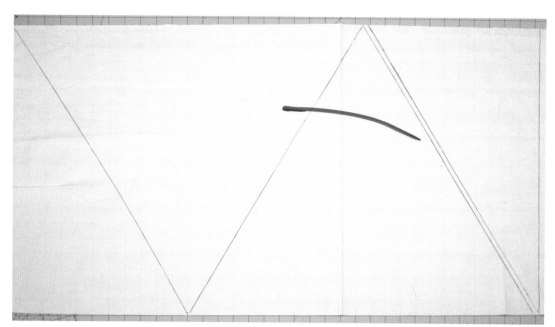

5. Draw a line ¼" (0.64cm) away from the line you just drew. Align the ruler to make a second half-equilateral triangle. Cut on the lines of the big triangles to make two large and two half-square equilateral triangles.

Ombré Star, page 68

Diamond, page 74

The Quilt Sandwich

The first time I heard the term "quilt sandwich" I just nodded my head and pretended I knew what it meant. It was one of the strangest terms I'd ever heard! Eventually, I learned it was a term to describe layering the quilt backing, batting, and quilt top. Making your quilt sandwich correctly is very critical to the outcome of your quilt.

Prepping the Quilt Top

Before I layer my quilt top, I carefully press it and then sew ⅛" (0.32cm) seam around the entire perimeter. The stitching acts like a stay stitch, ensuring the edges of the quilt stay square and straight before quilting. It also helps hold sewn seams together while quilting.

Prepping the Backing

Backing fabric should always measure 10" (25.40cm) wider than the quilt top to allow for shrinkage as you quilt. After quilting, any excess will be trimmed. The backing will either be pieced or 108" (274.32cm) fabric is available at some quilt shops to accommodate a seamless backing on your quilt.

Fabric requirements that include extra fabric for backing is included in the materials list for projects in the book. To prep your backing fabric, cut off selvages with a rotary cutter. Cut the backing fabric in as many equal widths as you need to span the quilt. With right sides together, sew the widths of fabric together along the cut sides, using a ¼" (0.64cm) seam. Press the seams open and press the backing fabric well.

Layering the Quilt Sandwich

Depending on the size of your quilt, you will need a large, flat area to lay out your backing, batting, and quilt top. I have a pair of 6' (182.88cm) tables and two sets of plastic bed risers I use to create my work surface. I place the tables side by side on top of the risers to raise the tables to counter height. Layers don't have to fit edge to edge on the surface. They can drape evenly off the sides of a table.

Lay the backing wrong side up on your work surface and smooth out any wrinkles. Use tape or binder clips to keep the backing in place.

Layer the bumpy side of the batting, facing up, on the quilt backing. Smooth out any wrinkles. (NOTE: If wrinkles are reluctant to smooth out, throw the batting in the dryer with a wet washcloth on low heat for a few minutes to reduce wrinkles.)

Center the quilt top over the backing and batting, making sure to smooth out all three layers as much as possible.

Pinning the Quilt Sandwich

If you are quilting on your home sewing machine, I recommend pin basting since it's the easiest way to keep layers in place. Start in the center of the quilt and pin every 6" (15.25cm) through all three layers. I prefer bent quilting pins to make it easier to rock into and out of the layers. If you are using your dining room table, take care not to poke pins into the surface.

Continue pinning, pulling the draped areas onto the table, and smoothing out the layers.

Quilting the Quilt

The process of quilting a quilt can and does merit its own book. In each quilt project, I discuss the quilting decisions that were made when deciding what design to use. I suggest making some small quilt sandwiches and practice stitching. When you are comfortable, you can start quilting your project.

Straight line quilting can be accomplished on your home machine using a walking foot. It always looks good and can be either simple or incredibly intricate. I teach first time quilters to sew straight lines about 2" (5.08cm) apart to secure the quilt layers. It creates a pleasing design and it's easy and functional at the same time. Quilt horizontally, vertically, or diagonally to create visual interest. You can create amazing texture by quilting very densely.

Continuous Binding

Congratulations! You pieced your top, you quilted your quilt and now it is time to bind. This is the piece of fabric that wraps around the raw edges of your quilt to hide the batting and secure the edges of your quilt. I always write my patterns to include 2½" (6.35cm) binding.

The following binding technique is a quilting standard through step 6. Step 7 is one of many ways to attach loose ends of the binding. To see my favorite technique with continuous binding, visit *www.quiltaddictsanonymous.com* for my tutorial, *How to Sew Binding on a Quilt.*

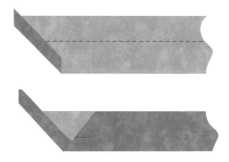

1. To sew the strips on the bias, arrange your binding strips right sides together at a right angle. Allow the selvages to hang past the edges of the strips. This will create two valleys that you will sew between. Pin the strips in place. Draw a line from valley to valley.

2. Sew on the line and trim the seam to ¼" (0.64cm). Press the seams to the side. Continue sewing the strips together in this manner to make one long strip. Fold with wrong sides together and press.

3. Unfold and trim one end of the strip to make a 45° angle. Turn under ½" (1.30cm), refold the strip and press the end.

4. Starting on the bottom of your quilt, lay the raw edge of binding even with the raw edge of your quilt top. Leaving about 6" (15.24cm) free, start sewing the binding to the edge of your quilt top through all three layers using a walking foot.

5. Stop with your needle down when you are ¼" (0.64cm) away from the edge of the first corner. Lift your presser foot and turn the quilt so the next edge is now facing you. Lift your needle up and gently pull the quilt out from under the presser foot a couple of inches. Don't cut the thread. Fold the binding back, aligning it with the raw edge of the quilt to form a 45° angle.

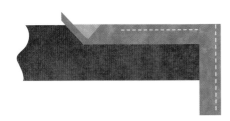 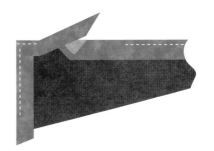 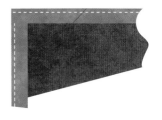

6. Refold the binding strip to align with the raw edge of the quilt top. Realign the quilt edge under the presser foot and continue sewing the binding to all sides of the quilt. Repeat steps 4 to 5 at each corner.

7. Stop stitching about 6" (17.15cm) from where you started attaching the binding. Trim the strip long enough to tuck the end into the angled binding piece. Make sure the binding lays flat and finish sewing the binding.

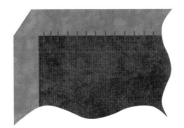 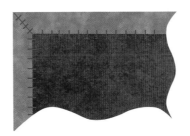 

8. Trim the backing and batting even with the quilt top, taking care not to cut into the binding, especially on the corners. Fold the binding to the back of the quilt. It should fit snug around the edges. Pin the binding in place. Hand stitch the binding to the quilt back and batting, taking ¼" (0.64cm) stitches. Fold 45° corners and stitch down, sewing along the fold to tack the corner down.

Label Your Quilt

I always label my quilts, including my name and the year the quilt was finished. You can include additional information, like who the quilt was gifted to, the name of the pattern, and the occasion it was given. Future generations will appreciate this information.

You can buy commercial labels, or make your own. Embroider the details if you like or use a permanent, color-fast pen to write the information.

With this last detail, you have completed your quilt!

Going North

Finished size: 60" x 77" (152.4 x 195.58cm)

Fabric Requirements

- ¼ yard (22.86cm) Fabric 1
- ¼ yard (22.86cm) Fabric 2
- ¼ yard (22.86cm) Fabric 3
- ¼ yard (22.86cm) Fabric 4
- 4 yards (365.76cm) Fabric 5
  (4½ yards [411.48cm] if your fabric is directional)
- 5 yards backing and batting

Cutting

From Fabric 1, cut:
(2) 2½" (6.35cm) x WOF strips

From Fabric 2, cut:
(2) 2½" (6.35cm) x WOF strips

From Fabric 3, cut:
(2) 2½" (6.35cm) x WOF strips

Fabric 4, cut:
(2) 2½" (6.35cm) x WOF strips

Fabric 5, cut:
(3) 6½" (16.51cm) x WOF strips. From the strips, cut:
    (14) 6½" (16.51cm) squares. Cut the squares
    diagonally to make (28) triangles.
    If you are using directional fabric, double the amount
    of strips, squares, and triangles.

(4) 6"(15.24cm) x WOF strips. From one strip, cut:
    (10) 3¼" x 6" (8.26 x 15.24cm) rectangles.
    From 2 strips, cut:
    (10) 6" (15.24cm) squares.

From one strip, cut:
(4) 6" x 8¾" (15.24 x 22.23cm) rectangles

(1) 77½" (196.85cm) x WOF strip. From the strip, cut:

    (1) 24¾" x 77½" (62.87 x 196.85cm) strip

    (1) 16½" x 77½" (41.91 x 196.85cm) strip

    (7) 2½" (6.35cm) x WOF strips for binding

Assembly Instructions

1. Layer a 2½" (6.35cm) strip from Fabric 1 and Fabric 2. Press seams open.

2. Repeat step 1 to make the following additional fabric strip combinations:
   - Fabrics 1 and 4
   - Fabrics 3 and 4
   - Fabrics 2 and 3

3. Refer to Cutting 90° Triangles on page 13 to make the following:
   Four each of:
   - Fabric 2 in the tip, Fabric 1 in the long strip
   - Fabric 4 in the tip, Fabric 1 in the long strip
   - Fabric 4 in the tip, Fabric 3 in the long strip
   - Fabric 2 in the tip, Fabric 3 in the long strip

4. Three each of:
   - Fabric 1 in the tip, Fabric 2 in the long strip
   - Fabric 1 in the tip, Fabric 4 in the long strip
   - Fabric 3 in the tip, Fabric 4 in the long strip
   - Fabric 3 in the tip, Fabric 2 in the long strip

5. With right sides together, layer triangles from Fabric 5 so that the long side aligns with the long side of a stripped triangle. Sew along the long side. Press seams open and trim to 6" (15.74cm) square.

Pro Tip:

Don't skip trimming the blocks down to 6" (15.20cm) square. Having crisp, perfectly square edges will make the final quilt assembly much easier and ensure you have a nice flat top when it comes time to quilt it.

6. Pair pieced half-square triangles together in colorways as shown. Sew together to make four each of the pieced flying geese units.

Make 4 of each

7. Pair pieced half-square triangles together in colorways as shown. Sew together to make three each of the pieced flying geese units.

Make 3 of each

8. Following the Center Panel Assembly Diagram, lay out the pieced flying geese units with 3¼" x 6" (8.26 x 15.24cm) rectangles, 6" x 8¾" (15.24 x 22.23cm) rectangles, and 6" (8.26cm) squares. Sew together to form rows as shown in Assembly Diagram 2. Sew the rows together to create the pieced center panel.

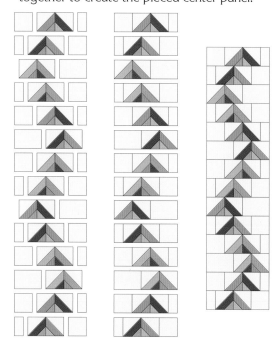

Center Panel Assembly Diagram

9. Arrange the 24¾" x 77½" (62.87 x 196.85cm) strip to the left of the pieced panel and the 16½" x 77½" (0.42 x1.97m) strip to the right of the pieced panel as shown in Quilt Top Assembly Diagram. Sew together to complete the quilt top.

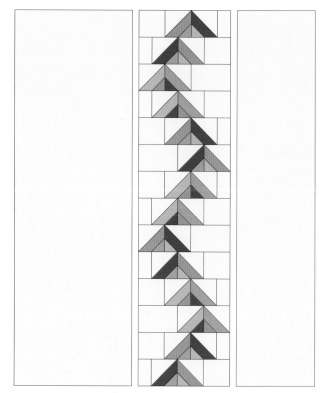

Quilt Top Assembly Diagram

Finishing the Quilt

1. Layer the quilt top, batting, and backing together. Refer to Stephanie's Quilting Designs (page 27) or quilt as desired.

2. Sew the binding strips together end-to-end, to make one long binding strip. Press seams open.

3. Press the strip wrong sides together. Sew it to the front of the quilt along the raw edges. Fold the binding over to the back, covering the raw edges and hand stitch in place.

NOTE: Refer to The Quilt Sandwich, page 20, and Continuous Binding, page 22.

Stephanie's Quilting Designs

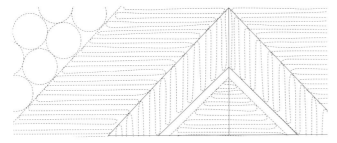

- For this quilt I asked award-winning quilter Natalia Bonner to bring the negative space to life, giving it texture that would add to the simple quilt design. In my opinion, before give your quilt to a long armer, you should trust their design style and their ability to use it to enhance your quilt design. I trust both with Natalia and she did not disappoint.

- She extended the design of the pieced flying geese with quilting, using a series of straight lines to bring the quilting design out further into the fabric flanking the pieced panel.

- To soften the angular look of the design, quilt circles across the remaining open space.

Quilting Suggestions

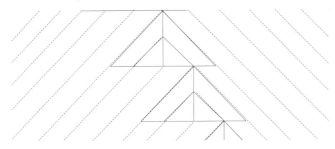

- Use your walking foot to quilt straight lines that converge at the points of the pieced flying geese. This would make every part of the quilt, including the texture of the quilting, point upward and to the center.

Houndstooth

Finished size: 96" x 108" (243.84 x 274.32cm)

Fabric Requirements

■ 2 yards (182.88cm) Fabric 1

■ 1¼ yard (114.30cm) Fabric 2

□ 1¼ yard (114.30cm) Fabric 3

■ 1¼ yard (114.30cm) Fabric 4

■ 1¼ yard (114.30cm) Fabric 5

■ 1¼ yards (114.30cm) Fabric 6

□ 5¼ yards (480.06cm) Fabric 7

9 yards (822.96cm) backing and batting

Cutting

From Fabric 1, cut:

(8) 2¾" (6.98cm) x WOF strips

(3) 6½" (16.51cm) x WOF strips. From the strips, cut: (18) 6½" (16.51cm) squares

(11) 2½" (6.35cm) x WOF strips for binding

From Fabric 2, cut:

(8) 2¾" (6.98cm) x WOF strips

(3) 6½" (16.51cm) x WOF strips. From the strips, cut: (17) 6½" (16.51cm) squares

From Fabric 3, cut:

(7) 2¾" (6.98cm) x WOF strips

(3) 6½" (16.51cm) x WOF strips. From the strips, cut: (13) 6½" (16.51cm) squares

From Fabric 4, cut:

(7) 2¾" (6.98cm) x WOF strips

(3) 6½" (16.51cm) x WOF strips. From the strips, cut: (13) 6½" (16.51cm) squares

From Fabric 5, cut:

(8) 2¾" (6.98cm) x WOF strips

(3) 6½" (16.51cm) x WOF strips. From the strips, cut: (13) 6½" (16.51cm) squares

From Fabric 6, cut:

(7) 2¾" (6.98cm) x WOF strips

(3) 6½" (16.51cm) x WOF strips. From the strips, cut: (15) 6½" (16.51cm) squares

From Fabric 7, cut:

(42) 2¾" (6.98cm) x WOF strips

(10) 6½" (16.51cm) x WOF strips. From strips cut: (56) 6½" (16.51cm) squares

Assembly Instructions

1. Sew one, 2¾" (7cm) x WOF Fabric 2 strip to one, 2¾" (7cm) x WOF Fabric 7 strip along the long side of strips. Press the seams open.

2. Referring to Cutting 90° Triangles on page 13, cut seven 90° triangles. The triangles will be a mirror image of each other. Make sure to alternate the direction of the first cut to balance the number of triangles.

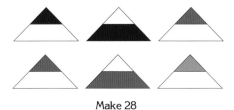

3. Repeat steps 1 and 2 with the remaining strips, pairing Fabrics 1 through 6 with Fabric 7. Make 28 mirrored sets of triangles from Fabrics 1, 2 and 6.

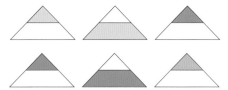

Make 28

For Fabrics 3, 4, and 5, make 24 of one mirror image triangle and 25 of its opposite. There will be extra triangles, so it doesn't matter which one has an extra.

Make 24 of one mirror image
and 25 of its opposite

4. Select a triangle where Fabric 1 is in the tip, and a second triangle where Fabric 2 is the long strip, as shown. Sew together, pressing seams open. Trim block to 6½" (16.51cm) square.

5. Repeat step 4 to make 13 of each block shown.
   - Fabric 1 in the corner, Fabric 2 in the long strip
   - Fabric 2 in the corner, Fabric 1 in the long strip
   - Fabric 1 in the corner, Fabric 6 in the long strip
   - Fabric 6 in the corner, Fabric 1 in the long strip

6. Repeat step 7 to make 11 of each block shown.
   - Fabric 3 in the corner, Fabric 2 in the long strip
   - Fabric 2 in the corner, Fabric 3 in the long strip
   - Fabric 4 in the corner, Fabric 3 in the long strip
   - Fabric 3 in the corner, Fabric 4 in the long strip
   - Fabric 5 in the corner, Fabric 6 in the long strip
   - Fabric 6 in the corner, Fabric 5 in the long strip
   - Fabric 4 in the corner, Fabric 5 in the long strip
   - Fabric 5 in the corner, Fabric 4 in the long strip

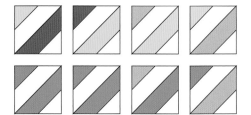

Pro Tip:
Don't skip trimming the blocks down to 6½" (16.51cm) square. You may only have a sliver of fabric to cut off, but having crisp, perfectly square edges will make the final quilt assembly much easier and ensure you have a nice flat top when it comes time to quilt it.

7. Referring to Assembly Diagram 1, layout the blocks with 6½" (16.51cm) squares from Fabrics 1 through 7. This process will be easiest if you lay the half-square triangles out on a design wall or a spare bed. If you have limited space, try laying out one row at a time on a long table.

Assembly Diagram 1

8. Referring to Assembly Diagram 2, sew the rows together as shown. Press the seams in odd rows to the left and even rows to the right. This will help your seams lock in place when you sew the rows together, creating perfect points.

Assembly Diagram 2

Finishing the Quilt

1. Layer the quilt top, batting, and backing together. Refer to Stephanie's Quilting Designs (page 33) or quilt as desired.

2. Sew the binding strips together end-to-end, to make one long binding strip. Press seams open.

3. Press the strip wrong sides together. Sew it to the front of the quilt along the raw edges. Fold the binding over to the back, covering the raw edges and hand stitch in place.

NOTE: Refer to The Quilt Sandwich, page 20, and Continuous Binding, page 22.

Stephanie's Quilting Designs

- An all-over linear pattern emphasizes the geometric design.

- Use straight line quilting, following the direction of the houndstooth blocks, and pointing to the upper left corner.

- Quilt straight lines in between the seams of each strip, creating a continuous line from the edge of the quilt to the center where the fabric colors meet. Choosing to quilt only in between the strips avoids having to stitch-in-the-ditch.

Quilting Suggestions

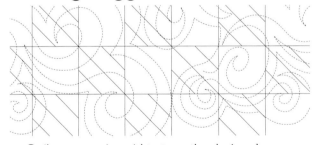

- Quilt an organic swirl to tone the design down.

- Use light gray, pale pink, yellow, green, and blue or light neutral threads when you want to use one thread across your entire quilt.

Ripples

Finished size: 66" x 96" (167.64 x 243.84cm)

Fabric Requirements

- 1½ yards (137.16cm) Fabric 1
- 1 yard (91.44cm) Fabric 2
- 1 yard (91.44cm) Fabric 3
- 1 yard (91.44cm) Fabric 4
- 1 yard (91.44cm) Fabric 5
- 3¾ yards (342.90cm) Fabric 6
- 6 yards (548.64cm) backing and batting

Cutting

From Fabric 1, cut:
(4) 7" (17.78cm) x WOF strips.
   From the strips, cut:
   (18) 7" (17.78cm) squares

(9) 2½" (6.35cm) by WOF strips for binding

From each of Fabrics 2, 3, and 4, cut:
(4) 7" (7.78cm) x WOF strips.
   From the strips, cut:
   (18) 7" (17.78cm) squares for a total of
   54 squares

From Fabric 5, cut:
(4) 7" (7.78cm) x WOF strips.
   From the strips, cut:
   (16) 7" squares

From Fabric 6, cut:
(18) 7" (7.78cm) x WOF strips.
   From the strips, cut:
   (88) 7" (7.78cm) squares

Assembly Instructions

1. With right sides together, layer one 7" (17.78cm) Fabric 6 square with a Fabric 4 square. Using a pencil, draw a line from corner-to-corner on the wrong side of Fabric 6.

2. Sew a scant ¼" (0.64cm) seam on each side of the drawn line. Cut the square apart on the drawn line to create two half-square triangles. Press the seams toward the darker fabric.

3. Trim the squares to 6½" (16.51cm) to create crisp, perfectly square edges.

> ### Pro Tip:
> Don't skip trimming the half-square triangles down to 6½" (16.51cm) square. You may only have a sliver of fabric to cut off, but having crisp, perfectly square edges will make the final quilt assembly much easier and ensure you have a nice flat top when it comes time to quilt it.

4. Repeat steps 1 through 4, pairing a Fabric 6 square with Fabrics 1 through 5. Sew to make (36) half-square triangles from Fabric 1 through 4, and (32) half-square triangles from Fabric 5.

| Make 36 | Make 32 |

Assembling the Quilt Top

1. Following Assembly Diagram 1, lay out the half-square triangles as shown.

NOTE: It's easiest to lay out the squares on a design wall or a spare bed. If your space is limited, lay out one row at time on a table. Be sure to label the rows.

2. Sew horizontal rows as shown in Assembly Diagram 2, pressing rows in opposite directions.

3. Sew the rows together into sets of two as shown in Assembly Diagram 3.

4. Continue sewing rows together in pairs, then sewing the pairs together to complete the quilt top.

Finishing the Quilt

1. Layer the quilt top, batting, and backing together. Refer to Stephanie's Quilting Designs (page 37) or quilt as desired.

2. Sew the binding strips together end-to-end to make one long binding strip. Press seams open.

3. Press the strip wrong sides together. Sew it to the front of the quilt along the raw edges. Fold the binding over to the back, covering the raw edges and hand stitch in place.

Assembly Diagram 1

Assembly Diagram 2

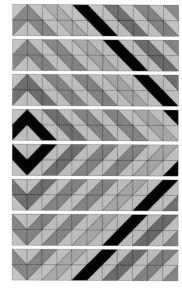

Assembly Diagram 3

Stephanie's Quilting Designs

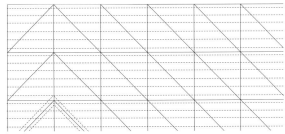

- Straight line quilt, sewing a horizontal stitching line every 1" (2.54cm) across the quilt to create texture, while letting the original design of the pattern show through. It emphasizes the diagonal lines going from right to left.

- Use light beige thread a shade or two lighter than Fabric 6 so the quilting blends into the background triangles and adds subtle definition to the prints.

Quilting Suggestions

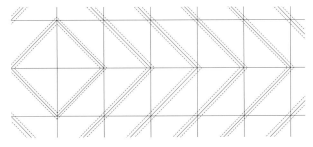

- Quilt swirls in the diamond ripples, matching the thread to the fabric you chose. This option would soften the sharp angles of the triangles by introducing curves and organic shapes.

- Try straight line quilting following the lines of the diagonals, so that the stitching echoes the design of the quilt. This would enhance geometric look of the design.

Herringbone

Finished size: 56" x 76" (142.24 x 190.50cm)

Fabric Requirements

2¾ yards (251.46cm) light gray fabric

1 yard (91.44cm) each 2 medium gray fabrics

1 yard (91.44cm) each 2 pink fabrics

1 yard (91.44cm) dark gray fabric

5 yards (457.20cm) backing fabric

Cutting

From light gray fabric, cut:
(52) 1½" (3.81cm) x WOF strips

(7) 2½" (6.35cm) x WOF strips for binding

From *each* of (2) medium gray fabrics, cut:
(12) 2½" (6.35cm) x WOF strips for a total of 24

From *each* of (2) pink fabrics, cut:
(12) 2½" (6.35cm) x WOF strips for a total of 24

From dark gray fabric, cut:
(12) 2½" (6.35cm) x WOF strips

Assembly Instructions

1. Select half of the strips from each fabric, arranging a 2½" (6.35cm) x WOF strip above the light gray 1½" (3.81cm) x WOF strip.

2. Cut a right angle triangle off the left side of half of the strips from each color way.

3. Sew together along the long sides, lining the angled edges up so the strips are offset. Sew together in the following order: medium gray, light gray, pink, light gray, dark gray, light gray, pink, light gray, medium gray, light gray. Press all seams open. Repeat to sew a total of (6) strip sets.

Make 6

4. Turn the pieced strip sets up as shown. Straighten the long edges, making sure the 45° line on the ruler is always even with the strip seams. Cut into 7½" (19.05cm) wide strips. You will get three from each strip set, for a total of 18.

Cut 18

5. Repeat steps 1 through 3, this time trimming the right angle triangle off the right side of the strips so the strip set angles in the opposite direction of the first strip set.

6. Repeat step 4, creating a total of 18 strip sets that are angled in the opposite direction of the strip sets in step 4.

7. Arrange strip sets from steps 4 and 6 in vertical rows as shown in Assembly Diagram 1. Sew together to form long vertical rows that point inward. You will have two strip sets left over from each direction.

Assembly Diagram 1

8. Sew the vertical rows together along the center to create four row sets as shown in Assembly Diagram 2. Be sure to offset the 2" (5.08cm) and 1" (2.54cm) strip points on the bottom as shown in Diagram 2.

Assembly Diagram 2

9. Sew the remaining four rows together and trim to straighten the top and bottom edges of the quilt top.

Finishing the Quilt

1. Layer the quilt top, batting, and backing together. Refer to Stephanie's Quilting Designs (page 41) or quilt as desired.

2. Sew the binding strips together end-to-end, to make one long binding strip. Press seams open.

3. Press strip wrong sides together. Sew it to the front of the quilt along the raw edges. Fold the binding over to the back, covering the raw edges and hand stitch in place.

NOTE: Refer to The Quilt Sandwich, page 20, and Continuous Binding, page 22.

Stephanie's Quilting Designs

- To emphasize the lines of piecing heading toward the center of the rows, use straight line quilting, stitching down the center of each strip.

- To make it fast and easy, start at the left side, stitch down the center of a strip to the row seam, travel down the center seam to the center of the next strip and repeat the process until reaching the right side of the quilt. Repeat with each strip.

- Use a light gray variegated thread for all the 2" (5.8cm) strips and a white thread for all of the 1" (2.54cm) strips. This way the fabric and the design are the stars of the show, not the quilting.

Quilting Suggestions

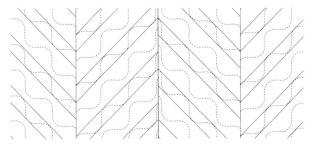

- You could easily accomplish the same on a domestic sewing machine with a walking foot.

- Other options could include straight line quilting vertically across the quilt. This would further enhance the appearance of the quilt to be pointing down.

- You could also use wavy lines with your free motion foot through the angled strips.

Bricks and Pavers

Finished size: 90" x 96" (228.60 x 243.84cm)

Fabric Requirements

2¾ yards (251.46cm) light gray fabric

⅔ yard (60.96cm) *each* of
6 assorted medium gray fabrics

⅔ yard (60.96cm) *each* of
4 assorted dark gray fabrics

⅔ yard (60.96cm) *each* of
2 assorted black fabrics

9 yards backing and batting

Cutting

From light gray fabric, cut:

(2) 6½" (16.51cm) x WOF strips.
     From the strips, cut:
     (24) 2½" x 6½" (6.35 x 16.51cm) rectangles

(3) 9½" (24.13cm) x WOF strips.
     From the strips, cut:
     (48) 2½" x 9½" (6.35 x 24.13cm) rectangles

(2) 12½" (31.75cm) x WOF strips.
     From the strips, cut:
     (24) 2½" x 12½" (6.35 x 31.75cm) rectangles

(10) 2½" (6.35cm) x WOF strips for binding

From each assorted medium gray fabric, cut:
(3) 6½" (16.51cm) x WOF strips

From each assorted dark gray fabric, cut:
(3) 6½" (16.51cm) x WOF strips

From each assorted black fabric, cut:
(3) 6½" (16.51cm) x WOF strips

Pro Tip:
Line an inch line on your ruler with the seam lines of your strip sets to make sure your seams are always at a 90° angle.

Assembly Instructions

1. Arrange three medium gray fabric 6½" (16.51cm) strips from lightest to darkest. Sew together along the long side of the strips to make an 18½" (47cm) x WOF strip panel. Press the seams open.

2. Repeat step 1 to make a total of three identical strip panels.

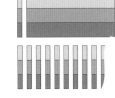

Make 3 strip sets

3. From each strip panel, cut 2½" x 18½" (6.35 x 47cm) strips to make a total of 48 strips. Set the strips aside and label as Strip Set 1.

4. Repeat steps 1 through 4 to create three additional strip sets. However, arrange the strips horizontally in the following order:

   • Strip Set 2: Dark gray, black, dark gray

   • Strip Set 3: Dark gray, dark gray, black

   • Strip Set 4: Medium gray, going from darkest to lightest.

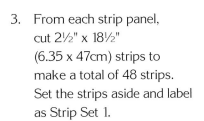

5. Arrange strip sets as shown, from left: Strip Set 1, Strip Set 2, Strip Set 3, and Strip Set 4.

6. Sew Strip Sets 1 and 2 together and 3 and 4 together, pressing the seams open. Sew the end of Strip Set 2 to the end of Strip Set 3, to form one long strip. Make a total of 48 Strip Sets.

Make 48 strip sets

7. Select 12 strip sets from step 6, (12) 2½" x 12½" (6.35 x 31.75cm) light gray strips, and (12) 2½" x 6½" (6.35 x 16.51cm) light gray strips. Sew the 2½" x 12½" (6.35 x 31.75cm) strips to the left side of the 12 strip sets and the 2½" x 6½" (6.35 x 16.51cm) strips to the right side of the strip sets. Press seams open.

8. Select 24 strip sets from step 6 and (48) 2½" x 9½" (6.35 x 24.13cm) light gray strips. Sew (24) 2½" x 9½" (6.35 x 24.13cm) strips to the left side of the strip sets and (24) 2½" x 9½" (6.35 x 24.13cm) strips to the right. Press seams open.

9. Select 12 strip sets from step 6, (12) 2½" x 6½" (6.35 x 16.51cm), and (12) 2½" x 12½" (6.35 x 31.75cm) light gray strips. Sew the 2½" x 6½" (6.35 x 16.51cm) strips to the left side of the strip set and the 2½" x 12½" (6.35 x 31.75cm) strips to the right. Press the seams open.

10. Arrange strip sets in the following order. The order refers to the first light gray strip in a row:
    - 2½" x 12½" (6.35 x 31.75cm)
    - 2½" x 9½" (6.35 x 24.13cm)
    - 2½" x 6½" (6.35 x 16.51cm)
    - 2½" x 9½" (6.35 x 24.13cm)
    Sew the rows together and press seams open.
    Make a total of (12) four-strip panel sections.

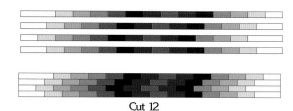

Cut 12

11. Starting with a 12½" (31.75cm) gray strip at the top left, lay out the strip sets made in step 10.

12. Sew the sets together in twos to make six strip sets. Press the seams open. Sew these sections together in sets of three, pressing the seams open.

13. Sew the final three sets together, pressing seams open to complete the quilt top.

Finishing the Quilt

1. Layer the quilt top, batting, and backing together. Refer to Stephanie's Quilting Designs (page 45) or quilt as desired.

2. Sew the binding strips together end-to-end to make one long binding strip. Press the seams open.

3. Press the strip wrong sides together. Sew it to the front of the quilt along the raw edges. Fold the binding over to the back, covering the raw edges and hand stitch in place.

NOTE: Refer to The Quilt Sandwich, page 20, and Continuous Binding, page 22.

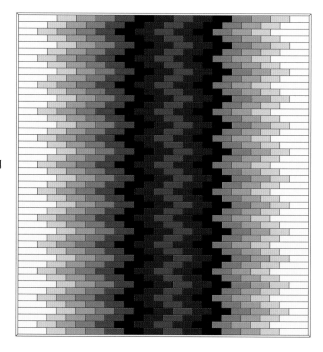

Stephanie's Quilting Designs

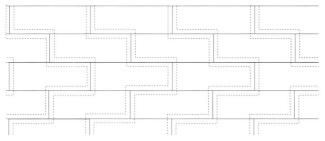

- Outline the quilt to create quilting lines that run a ¼" (0.64cm) away from both sides of the seam line. The texture of the quilting mimics the quilt design, accentuating the staggered look even more.

- Sew along the horizontal seam until the edge of the sewing foot is even with the edge of the next vertical seam. If you're using a ruler to guide you, pause with the needle down, move the ruler even with the next vertical seam, and stitch up. Continue in this manner, changing direction with each seam, always keeping the edge of the sewing foot a ¼" (0.64cm) away from the seam line.

- Use one light gray variegated thread for the entire quilt. It is easier for a light thread to disappear in a dark fabric, than a dark thread on the light fabric. The dark thread will always stand out, but the light will blend with the print.

Quilting Suggestions

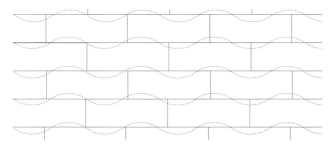

- Try horizontal or vertical lines.

- Wavy lines would be a fast, easy alternative to straight line quilting. The constant undulating motion of the quilting stitches will help soften the graphic lines of the quilt pattern.

Stripes

Finished size: 60" x 72" (152.40 x 182.88cm)

Fabric Requirements

- ⅔ yard (60.95cm) Fabric 1
- 1¼ yards (114.30cm) Fabric 2
- 1¼ yard (114.30cm) Fabric 3
- ½ yard (45.72cm) Fabric 4
- 1¾ yards (160.02cm) Fabric 5
- 4 yards (365.76cm) backing and batting

Cutting

From Fabric 1, cut:
(6) 3½" (8.89cm) x WOF strips

From Fabric 2, cut:
(6) 6½" (16.51cm) x WOF strips

From Fabric 3, cut:
(7) 3½" (8.89cm) x WOF strips
   From the strips, cut:
   (4) 3½" x 36½" (8.89 x 92.71cm) strips
(7) 2½" (6.35cm) x WOF strips for binding

From Fabric 4, cut:
(2) 6½" (16.51cm) x WOF strips
   From the strips, cut:
   (2) 6½" x 36½" (16.51 x 92.71cm) strips

From Fabric 5, cut:
(2) 30½" (77.73cm) x WOF strips
   From strips, cut:
   (1) 30½" x 36½" (77.73cm x 92.71cm) strip
   (1) 12½" x 30½" (31.75 x 77.73cm) strip

Pro Tip:

This quilt gives you a great opportunity to use some of the large scale quilting prints that are just too pretty to cut up into tiny pieces.

Assembly Instructions

1. Lay out two Fabric 1 strips, two Fabric 2 strips, and one Fabric 3 strip. Sew strips together to make a 21½" (54.61cm) x WOF strip set. Press the seams open.

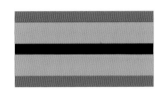

2. Repeat to make a total of 3 strip sets. Trim 2 sets to measure 21½" x 36½" (54.61 x 92.71cm). Press the seams open.

3. Trim the third strip set to make two 12½" x 21½" (31.75cm x 54.61cm) strip sets. Press the seams open.

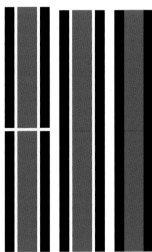

4. Lay out (4) Fabric 3 strips and (2) Fabric 4 strips as shown.

5. Sew the Fabric 3 strips together, pressing the seams in the same direction.

6. Sew the Fabric 4 strips together, pressing seams in the opposite direction of the Fabric 3 strips.

7. Sew the Fabric 3 strips to either side of the Fabric 4 strips. Press the seams open.

Quilt Assembly

1. Lay out the quilt strips and panels as shown in Assembly Diagram 1.

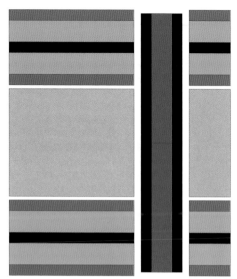

Assembly Diagram 1

2. Sew the 30½" x 36½" (77.47 x 92.71cm) strip sets to the top and bottom of Fabric 5 panel. Press the seams open.

3. Sew the 12½" x 21½" (31.75 x 54.61cm) strips to the top and bottom of the Fabric 5 panel. Press the seams open.

4. Sew the sections together from steps 2 and 3 to complete the quilt top. Press the seams open.

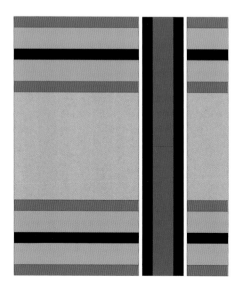

Finishing the Quilt

1. Layer the quilt top, batting, and backing together. Refer to Stephanie's Quilting Designs (page 49) or quilt as desired.

2. Sew the binding strips together end-to-end to make one long binding strip. Press the seams open.

3. Press the strip wrong sides together. Sew it to the front of the quilt along the raw edges. Fold the binding over to the back, covering the raw edges and hand stitch in place.

NOTE: Refer to The Quilt Sandwich, page 20, and Continuous Binding, page 22.

Stephanie's Quilting Designs

- Sometimes when you are deciding how to quilt a quilt, the fabric will tell you what to do. In this case, there were lots of lines in the fabric that I could follow with my quilting designs to help make my fabric choices stand out even more.

- For the 6½" (16.51cm) horizontal multicolored striped fabric strips, quilt following the lines of the stripes. To create additional texture, choose a hot pink thread that blends in with the colors in that print.

- Too accentuate the diagonal lines in the black and white 3½" (8.89cm) strips, use black thread and quilt in between every other diagonal line on the fabric.

- Using white thread, quilt horizontal lines, staying in between the black squares, and stitching across the large black/white check sections.

- Quilt the small gray/black vertical lines going up and down the teal stripes, using variegated thread and quilting every 1" (2.54cm) in the center stripe. This dark color blends wonderfully with the darker lines in the print.

- Since there was no obvious design in the magenta fabric, quilt diagonal lines to mimic the diagonal lines in the black stripes, carrying the design throughout the quilt. Use a thread that matches perfectly, so you just see texture, not bold thread staring back at you.

Quilting Suggestions

- Let your quilt tell you how it wants to be quilted. Since the fabric choices for this quilt were very geometric, your quilting choices could be completely different.

  For example, some of the large modern floral blooms would look great in place of the large horizontal center stripe. Then you may want to consider outlining the design of the flowers to accentuate the motif of the floral design.

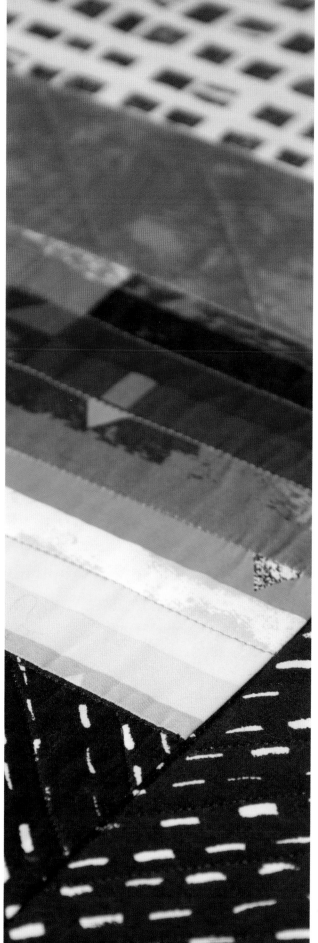

Ombré

Finished size: 66" x 78" (167.64 x 198.12cm)

Fabric Requirements

- 3¼ yards (297.18cm) Fabric 1
- ¼ yard (22.86cm) Fabric 2
- ¼ yard (22.86cm) Fabric 3
- ¼ yard (22.86cm) Fabric 4
- ¼ yard (22.86cm) Fabric 5
- ¼ yard (22.86cm) Fabric 6
- ¼ yard (22.86cm) Fabric 7
- ¼ yard (22.86cm) Fabric 8
- ¼ yard (22.86cm) Fabric 9
- ¼ yard (22.86cm) Fabric 10
- 5 yards (4457.20cm) backing fabric

Pro Tip:

When selecting fabric, pick colors that gradually change from one hue to another to create subtle contrast. Keep the same dark, bold color in the center of each row. It will give the eye a place to rest as the colors change throughout each row of the quilt.

Cutting

From Fabric 1, cut:

(14) 6½" (16.51cm) x WOF strips.
  From the strips, cut:
  (4) 6½" x 39½" (16.51 x 100.33cm) strips
  (7) 6½" x 43" (16.51 x 109.22cm) strips
  From 3 strips, cut:
  (7) 6½" x 12" (16.51 x 30.48cm) strips

(8) 2½" (6.35cm) x WOF strips for binding

From Fabric 2 to 10, cut:

(1) 6½" (16.51cm) x WOF strip from each color for a total of (9) strips

Assembly instructions

1. Sew the Fabric 2 and 3, 6½" (16.51cm) x WOF strips together along the long side. Press the seams open.

2. Sew the Fabric 4, 6½" (16.51cm) x WOF strip to Fabric 3 along the long side. Press the seams open.

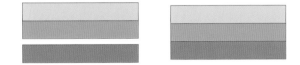

3. Continue adding 6½" (16.51cm) x WOF strips to the strip set. Add strips in order starting with Fabric 5 and ending with Fabric 10. Press the seams open.

4. From the strip set, cut a 6½" (16.51cm) strip by the length of the set to make a 6½" x 54½" (16.51 x 138.43cm) strip set of nine fabrics. Continue cutting to make a total of (6) 6½" x 54½" (16.51 x 138.43cm) strip sets.

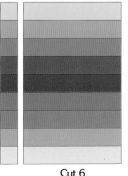

Cut 6

5. Sew (1), 6½" x 43" (16.51 x 109.22cm) Fabric 1 strip to (1) 6½" x 12" (16.51 x 30.48cm) Fabric 1 strip along the 6½" (16.51cm) side, pressing seams open. Repeat to create (7), 6½" x 54½" (16.51 x 138.43m) strips.

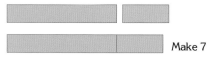

Make 7

6. With Fabric 10 on the left, layer the strip set on top of a Fabric 1 strip. Sew together, pressing the seams open. Repeat to make 3 sets.

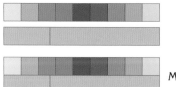

Make 3

7. With Fabric 2 on the left, layer the strip set on top of a Fabric 1 strip. Sew together, pressing the seams open. Repeat to make 3 sets.

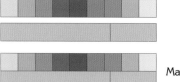

Make 3

8. Arrange the rows as shown in Assembly Diagram 1 alternating Fabric 1 and Fabric 10 ombré colorways to start the rows.

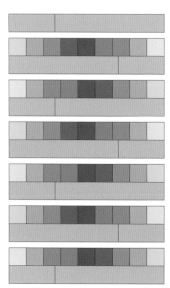

Assembly Diagram 1

9. Sew the rows together and press the seams open to finish the quilt center.

10. Sew (2) 6½" x 39½" (16.51 x 100.33cm) Fabric 1 strips together along the 6½" (16.51cm) side. Press the seams open. Repeat to make (2) Fabric 1 sets.

11. Sew a strip set from step 10 to each side of the quilt center, pressing the seams open to finish the quilt top.

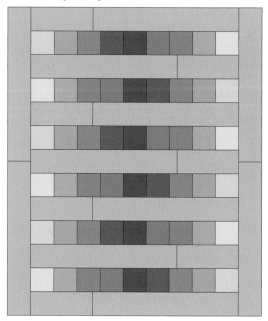

Finishing the Quilt

1. Layer the quilt top, batting, and backing together. Refer to Stephanie's Quilting Designs (page 53) or quilt as desired.

2. Sew the binding strips together end-to-end, to make one long binding strip. Press the seams open.

3. Press the strip wrong sides together. Sew it to the front of the quilt along the raw edges. Fold the binding over to the back, covering the raw edges and hand stitch in place.

NOTE: Refer to The Quilt Sandwich, page 20, and Continuous Binding, page 22.

Stephanie's Quilting Designs

Pro Tip:
The quilting design on Ombré is very minimal and spaced far apart in some places. To prevent the batting from shifting over time, make sure you choose a batting that allows you to space the quilting apart. Some battings only allow for quilting spaced up to 3" (7.62cm) apart, and that would not work for a minimalist quilting design like this one.

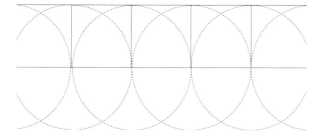

- Quilt 12" (30.48cm) circles across the top of the quilt.

- On the Fabric 1 background rows, match the thread color to the fabric. In order to avoid having to switch quilting thread in the middle of each circle, quilt a line of half circles across each background row in the matching thread.

- To quilt the strip pieced rows, switch to thread that matches the lighter of the fabrics in the design quilting the bottom half of the circles in the same manner as before.

Quilting Suggestions

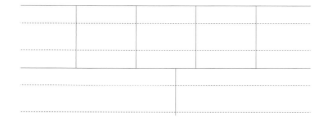

- Use straight line quilting with matching thread in the background Fabric 1 rows. Then use a variety of threads to match the colors in the ombré strip in the strip set rows. This would add depth, dimension, and carry the horizontal design through from the piecing to the quilting texture.

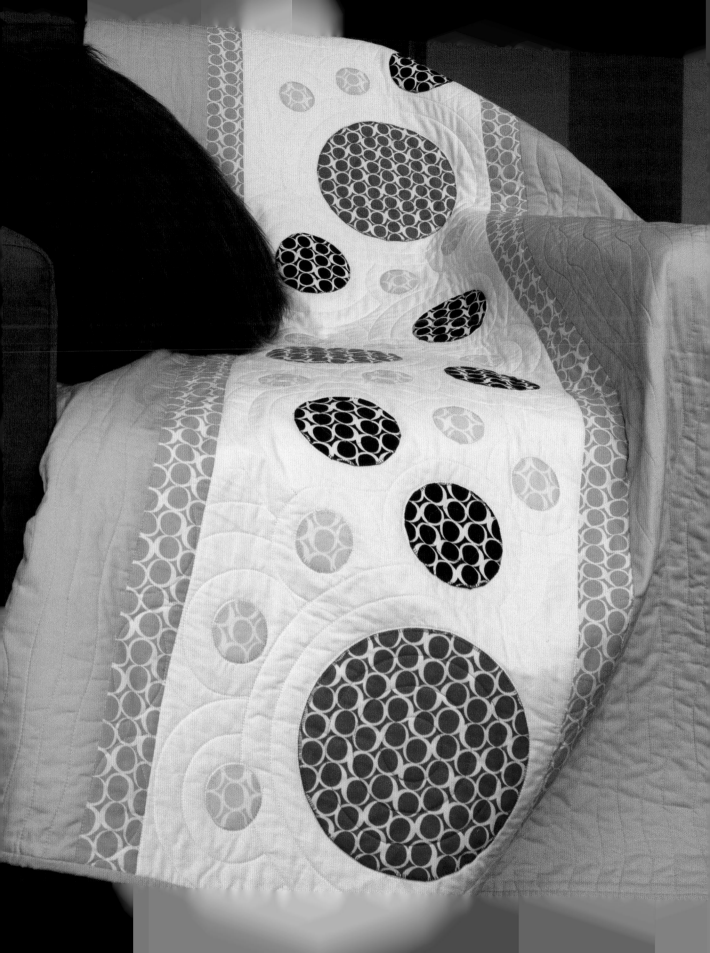

Bubbles

Finished size: 58" x 84" (147.32 x 213.36cm)

Fabric Requirements

- 3 yards (274.32cm) Fabric 1
- ½ yard (45.72cm) Fabric 2
- 1¼ yard (114.30cm) Fabric 3
- ¼ yard (22.86cm) Fabric 4
- ¼ yard (22.86cm) Fabric 5
- ¼ yard (22.86cm) Fabric 6
- ¼ yard (22.86cm) Fabric 7
- 5¼ yards (480.06cm) backing and batting

Cutting

From Fabric 1, cut:
(1) 84½" (214.63cm) x WOF strip. From the strip, cut:
   (1) 30¼" x 84½" (76.85 x 214.63cm) piece
   (1) 10¼" x 84½" (26.04 x 214.63cm) piece
(8) 2½" (6.35cm) x WOF strips for binding

From Fabric 2, cut:
(6) 2½" (6.35cm) x WOF strips. From the strips, cut:
   (6) 2½" x 28½" (6.35 x 72.38cm) strips

From Fabric 3, cut:
(3) 14½" (36.83cm) x WOF strips. From the strips, cut:
   (3) 14½" x 28½" (36.83 x 72.38cm) strips

From Fabric 4, cut:
(1) 8½" (21.59cm) x WOF strip. From the strip, cut:
   (3) 8½" (21.59cm) squares

From Fabric 5, cut:
(1) 6½" (16.51cm) x WOF strip. From the strip, cut:
   (2) 6½" (16.51cm) squares

From Fabric 6, cut:
(1) 4½" (11.43cm) x WOF strip. From the strip, cut:
   (8) 4½" (11.43cm) squares

From Fabric 7, cut:
(2) 2½" (6.35cm) x WOF strips. From the strips, cut:
   (20) 2½" (6.35cm) squares

Assembly Instructions

1. Using the template on page 58, trace three, 8" (20.32cm) circles on the paper side of the fusible web. (I like Heat n' Bond®) Draw a line, ¼" (0.64cm) away from both sides of the traced line.

2. Cut out the center of the paper, leaving the ¼" (0.64cm) lines.

3. Following the manufacturer's instructions, iron the fusible web to the wrong side of a Fabric 4, 8½" (21.59cm) square.

4. Allow the fusible web to cool, then cut the fabric circle out on the drawn line to make three, 8" (20.32cm) Fabric 4 circles.

Make 3

5. Repeat steps 1 through 4 with the remaining circle templates. Cut:
   - Two, 6" (15.24cm) circles from Fabric 5
   - Eight, 4" (10.16cm) circles from Fabric 6
   - Twenty, 2" (5.08cm) circles from Fabric 7
   Set circles aside, leaving paper backing intact.

Make 2   Make 8   Make 20

6. Referring to Panel Assembly Diagram, sew the Fabric 2, 2½" x 28½" (6.35 x 72.39cm) strips end-to-end to make 2, 2½" x 84½" (6.35 x 214.63cm) strips. Press the seam in one direction.

7. Repeat step 6 with the 14½" x 28½" (36.83 x 72.39cm) strips from Fabric 3 to make one, 14½" x 84½" (36.83 x 214.63cm) piece. Press the seams in the opposite direction of the seams in step 6.

8. Sew the Fabric 2 strips to both sides of the Fabric 3 strip. Press the seams under Fabric 2. The seams will lock in place because they are pressed in opposite directions, making it easier to have perfect seam joins.

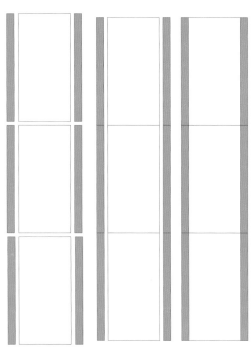

Panel Assembly Diagram

9. Arrange the circles on top of the Fabric 3 panel as shown. Remove the paper backing from the circles, one at a time, and iron in place, following the manufacturer's instructions. Sew a decorative stitch around the edge of each circle to secure it to the background fabric. My favorite is the buttonhole stitch.

Pro Tip:

When you are fusing the circles to the panel, use a flat pressing surface, like an ironing mat, instead of an ironing board. That way you can work on a large table top, sliding the mat under the panel as you work. This makes it much easier to keep the circles in place, than it would be on an ironing board.

By cutting the inside of the fusible web out, leaving just the ¼" (0.64cm) inside the template line, your appliqué will be much softer and more flexible. That will make it feel more like hand appliqué, even though you took the fast, simple route and used fusible appliqué.

10. Sew the 30¼" x 84½" (76.84 x 214.63cm) strip from Fabric 1 to the left side of the circle panel, as shown in Assembly Diagram 1. Press the seams under Fabric 1.

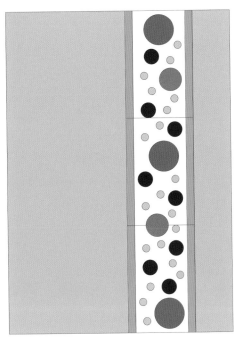

Assembly Diagram 1

11. Sew the 10¼" x 84½" (26.03 x 214.63cm) strip from Fabric 1 to the right side of the circle panel. Press the seams under Fabric 1 to complete the quilt top.

Finishing the Quilt

1. Layer the quilt top, batting, and backing together. Refer to Stephanie's Quilting Designs (page 59) or quilt as desired.

2. Sew the binding strips together end-to-end to make one long binding strip. Press the seams open.

3. Press the strip wrong sides together. Sew it to the front of the quilt along the raw edges. Fold the binding over to the back, covering the raw edges and hand stitch in place.

NOTE: Refer to The Quilt Sandwich, page 20, and Continuous Binding, page 22.

Print 4

Enlarge 120%

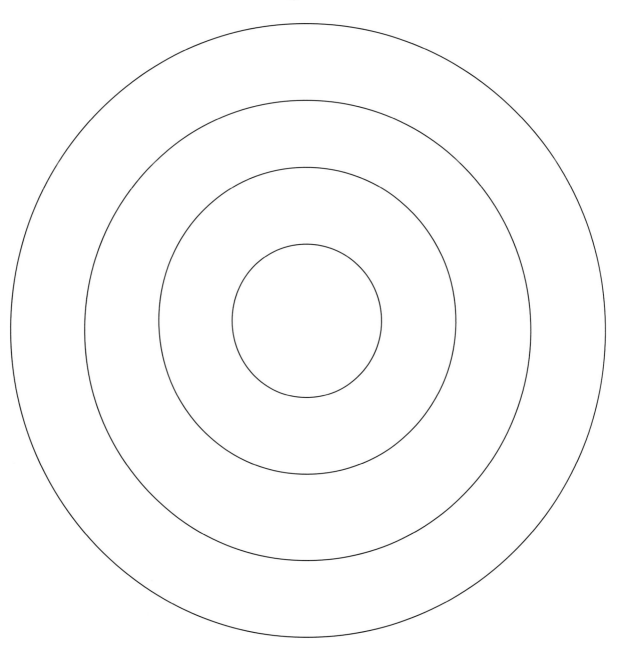

Stephanie's Quilting Designs

- Create a ghost quilting design in the negative space of this quilt, replicating the circle design.

- Echo the circle design, creating larger and larger circles until the panel is filled.

- Quilt wavy lines to make it look like water around bubbles, in between and on the sides of the appliqué and ghost circle panel. Don't use a template. That is the beauty of wavy lines. Just create long, smooth curves that are completely random.

- Match the thread to the fabric as closely as possible. That way the design and texture will stand out.

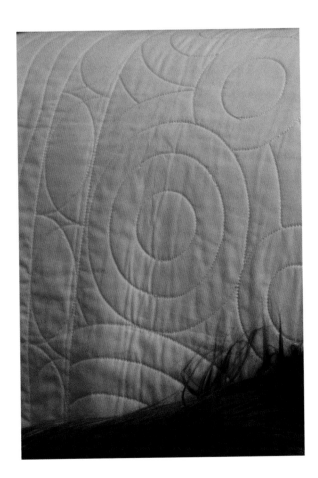

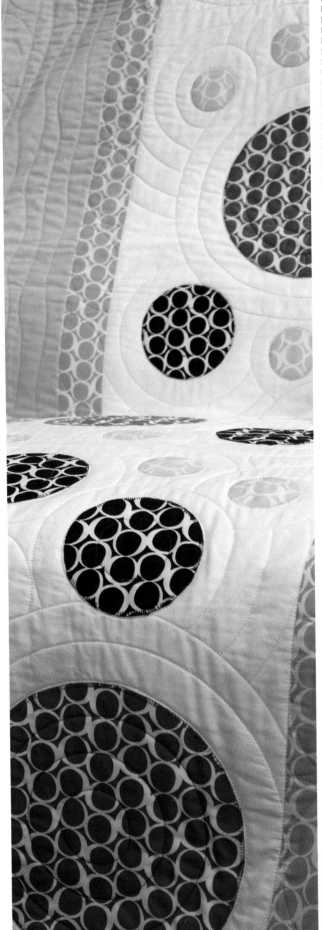

On the 60

Finished size: 70" x 96" (177.80 x 243.84cm)

Fabric Requirements

- 1¾ yards (160.02cm) Fabric 1
- 1¾ yards (160.02cm) Fabric 2
- 1¾ yards (160.02cm) Fabric 3
- 2½ yards (228.60cm) Fabric 4
- 6 yards (548.64cm) backing and batting

Cutting

Refer to Cutting Triangles, page 12. Set aside the half triangles for row setting triangles. Make sure to leave ¼" (0.64cm) seam allowance when cutting left and right triangles horizontally.

From Fabric 1, cut:

(9) 6¾" (17.15cm) x WOF strips. From the strips, cut:
   (9) 6¾" (17.15cm) triangles,
   (1) left half-square triangle
   (1) right half-square triangle

From Fabric 2, cut:

(9) 6¾" (17.15cm) x WOF strips. From the strips, cut:
   (9) 6¾" (17.15cm) triangles,
   (1) left half-square triangle
   (1) right half-square triangle

From Fabric 3, cut:

(9) 6¾" (17.15cm) x WOF strips. From the strips, cut:
   (9) 6¾" (17.15cm) triangles,
   (1) left half-square triangle
   (1) right half-square triangle

From Fabric 4, cut:

(9) 6¾" (17.15cm) x WOF strips. From the strips, cut:
   (9) 6¾" (17.15cm) triangles,
   (1) left half-square triangle
   (1) right half-square triangle

(8) 2½" (6.35cm) x WOF strips for binding.

NOTE: You will need a total of 76 triangles,
   (4) left half-square triangles
   (4) right half-square triangles from each fabric

Assembly Instructions

1. The fabric order for the rows are as follows:
   - Row 1: Fabric 4, Fabric 1, Fabric 2, Fabric 3
   - Row 2: Fabric 1, Fabric 2, Fabric 3, Fabric 4
   - Row 3: Fabric 2, Fabric 3, Fabric 4, Fabric 1
   - Row 4: Fabric 3, Fabric 4, Fabric 1, Fabric 2

You will need to make four of each row.

2. Select a half-triangle from Fabric 4, and one triangle each from Fabrics 1, 2, and 3.

3. With right sides together, align the points by placing Fabric 4 over Fabric 1 and Fabric 2 over Fabric 3. Sew, using a ¼" (0.64cm) seam. Sew the two sections together to start row 1.

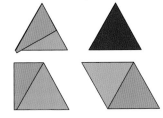

4. Press the seams open. Continue sewing triangles in this manner to create quilt rows. Make sure half-square triangles are mirrored at either end of a row.

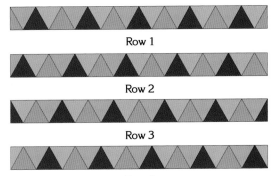

Row 1

Row 2

Row 3

Row 4

5. Following the Assembly Diagram to create 4 sections of rows 1, 2, 3, and 4. Press seams open.

Assembly Diagram

6. Sew the 4 row sections together to complete the quilt top. Press the seams open.

Finishing the Quilt

1. Layer the quilt top, batting, and backing together. Refer to Stephanie's Quilting Designs (page 63) or quilt as desired.

2. Sew the binding strips together end-to-end to make one long binding strip. Press the seams open.

3. Press the strip wrong sides together. Sew it to the front of the quilt along the raw edges. Fold the binding over to the back, covering the raw edges and hand stitch in place.

NOTE: Refer to The Quilt Sandwich, page 20, and Continuous Binding, page 22.

Pro Tip:

By pressing the triangle seams open and not trimming the dog ears, you can line up the next triangle with the point in the seam allowance to get perfect piecing.

In order to get perfect points when you sew the triangles together, put a pin directly through the seams of the joining triangles a ¼" (0.64cm) from the side of the block.

Pinch the fabric right next to the pin, so the pin is held firmly in place, perpendicular to the fabric. Take a second pin and pin the seam in place before removing the first pin. This will help ensure your points stay in place.

Stephanie's Quilting Designs

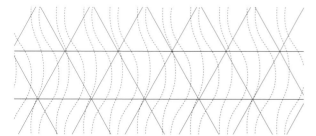

- Quilt simple wavy lines from top to bottom.

- Sew five wavy lines per triangle.

- The curves on the wavy lines are all random and undulate without any rules or pattern.

Quilting Suggestions

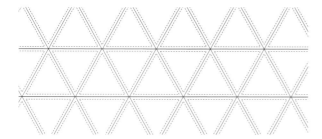

- Stitch ¼" (0.64cm) away from both sides of each seam with a walking foot to emphasize the triangle design.

- Quilt arcs inside each triangle to soften the angular design of the quilt.

- Quilt free motion swirls, feathers, flames, or just about any design inside each triangle.

Argyle

Finished size: 89¼" x 97½" (226.70 x 247.78cm)

Fabric Requirements

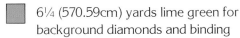 6¼ (570.59cm) yards lime green for background diamonds and binding

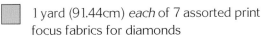 1 yard (91.44cm) *each* of 7 assorted print focus fabrics for diamonds

8⅓ yards (761.97cm) backing and batting

Cutting

Refer to Cutting Diamonds, page 12.

From lime green fabric, cut:

(28) 7" (17.78cm) x WOF strips.
    From the strips, cut:
    (112) diamonds

(10) 2½" (6.35cm) x WOF strips for binding

From *each* of the 7 focus fabrics, cut:

(4) 7" (17.78cm) x WOF strips. From each strip, cut:
    (4) 7" (17.78cm) diamonds for a total of
      16 per print

Pro Tip:

In order to get perfect points when you sew the diamonds together, put a pin directly through the edge of the joining diamonds, ¼" (0.64cm) from the side of the pieces.

Hold the pieces firmly and place the pin perpendicular to the fabric. Repeat with a second pin. This will ensure your points stay in place.

Assembly Instructions

1. Select 16 lime green diamonds, align a ruler vertically and to the right of center on the ¼" (0.64cm) line as shown. Cut to make (16) side setting triangles.

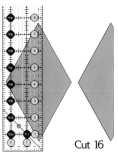

Cut 16

2. Select 4 side setting triangles from Step 1, layer 2 sides together. Align a ruler vertically and to the right of center on the ¼" (0.64cm) line as shown. Cut to make 4 mirrored diamonds for quilt corners.

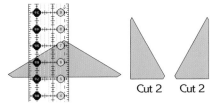

Cut 2   Cut 2

3. From each of 24 lime green diamonds, align a ruler vertically and to the right of center on the ¼" (0.64cm) line as shown. Cut to make 24 top and bottom setting triangles.

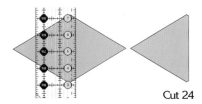

Cut 24

4. Following Assembly Diagram 1, lay out the diamonds in rows. Use one color of a focus fabric for each row.

Assembly Diagram 1

5. Following Assembly Diagram 2, sew the diamonds together in diagonal rows, using a ¼" (0.64cm) seam allowance.

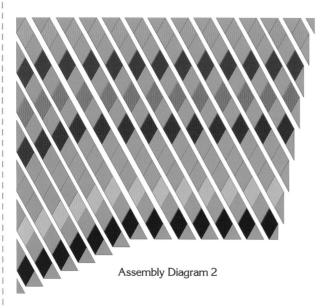

Assembly Diagram 2

6. Sew the rows together to complete the quilt top.

Finishing the Quilt

1. Layer the quilt top, batting, and backing together. Refer to Stephanie's Quilting Designs (page 67) or quilt as desired.

2. Sew the binding strips together end-to-end to make one long binding strip. Press the seams open.

3. Press the strip wrong sides together. Sew it to the front of the quilt along the raw edges. Fold the binding over to the back, covering the raw edges and hand stitch in place.

NOTE: Refer to The Quilt Sandwich, page 20, and Continuous Binding, page 22.

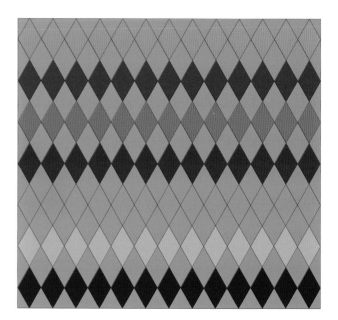

Stephanie's Quilting Designs

- Outline all of the diamonds with stitch-in-the-ditch quilting, using thread to match the background fabric.

- Quilt from left to right, starting at the edge of the quilt, first stitching the top half of the diamond to the right end of the row. Start over, sewing the quilt from left to right, stitching the bottom edge of the diamond.

- Sew large arcs in the focus prints working from left to right, quilting one-half of the diamond at a time to sew one continuous line from one side of the quilt to the other.

- Quilt free motion swirls in the background diamonds to add some texture and mimic the swirl design in the fabric.

Quilting Suggestions

- Straight line quilt following the 60° lines of the diamonds.

- Cross in both directions to create a criss-cross effect emphasizing, the argyle pattern.

Ombré Star

Finished size: 66" x 74" (167.64 x 187.96cm)

Fabric Requirements

¾ yard (68.58cm) of six colors of gradated fabrics: (Gradated fabrics subtly shift colors across the width of fabric)

1 yard (91.44cm) light gray background fabric

3 yards (274.32cm) light gray background fabric

4¼ yards (388.62cm) backing and batting

Cutting

From each of 6 gradated color fabric pieces, and cutting parallel to the selvage, cut:
(7) 5½" x 27" (13.97 x 68.58cm) strips

NOTE: I suggest cutting the first strip in the center, across the fold of the fabric. Work from the center, out, to cut additional strips.

From the gray gradated fabric, and cutting parallel to the selvage, cut:
(7) 5½" x 36" (13.97 x 91.44cm) strips

From background fabric, cut:
(4) 19½" (49.53cm) by WOF strips

(8) 2½"(6.35cm) by WOF strips for binding

Assembly Instructions

Refer to Cutting Triangles on page 12.

1. From each of six colors, cut up to four triangles from each strip. You will cut 28 triangles from each fabric color. Keep them organized according to the color change to make assembling the diamond easier.

Cut 28

2. From the light gray gradated fabric, cut eight triangles from each strip, for a total of 56 triangles. Keep them organized according to the color change to make assembling the diamond easier.

Cut 56

3. Arrange the colored triangles, and the light gray triangles from light to dark, as shown. You will have two extra dark triangles and two extra light triangles.

4. With right sides together, sew the triangles into diamonds.

Pro Tip:

In order to get perfect points when you sew the diamonds together, put a pin directly through the edge of the joining diamonds, ¼" (0.64cm) from the side of the pieces.

Hold the pieces firmly and place the pin perpendicular to the fabric. Repeat with a second pin. This will ensure your points stay in place.

5. With right sides together, sew the diamonds into rows.

6. Sew the rows together to complete a diamond.

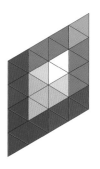

7. Repeat steps 3 through 8 with the remaining gradated fabrics to create a total of six pieced diamonds.

Cutting Large Background Triangles

Refer to page 18 to cut triangles for this quilt.

For this step, you will need to mark lines with a pencil or a FriXion™ Gel Pen. It's my favorite marking tool! The marks from it can be removed with steam if you make a mistake and need to "erase" a line. You will also need a 6" x 24" (15.24 x 60.96cm) ruler with 30° and 60° lines.

1. Prepare the four, 19½" (49.53cm) by WOF strips from the background fabric by cutting off the selvages to square up the edges of each piece. Draw a ¼" (0.64cm) line from the cut edge across the width of each strip.

2. Working with one strip at a time, mark the strip to create two half-equilateral triangles and two 60° triangles.

3. Repeat the step-by-step for the remaining fabric strips. You will cut a total of eight equilateral triangles and eight half-equilateral triangles.

Cut 8 of each triangle shape

Quilt Assembly

1. Referring to Assembly Diagram 1, arrange the diamonds from step 6 and the large triangles from step 12 as shown.

Assembly Diagram 1

2. Sew the quilt into wedges, first adding the large triangles to the diamonds, then adding the half-equilateral triangles as shown in Assembly Diagram 2.

Assembly Diagram 2

3. Sew the wedges together to make top and bottom halves as shown in Assembly Diagram 3.

4. Sew the halves together to complete the quilt top.

Assembly Diagram 3

Finishing the Quilt

1. Layer the quilt top, batting, and backing together. Refer to Stephanie's Quilting Designs (page 73) or quilt as desired.

2. Sew the binding strips together end-to-end to make one long binding strip. Press the seams open.

3. Press the strip wrong sides together. Sew it to the front of the quilt along the raw edges. Fold the binding over to the back, covering the raw edges and hand stitch in place.

Stephanie's Quilting Designs

- Starting with the background, outline the star by stitching in the ditch in thread that matches the background fabric. Stitch ½" (1.30cm) away from the star and 1" (2.50cm) away from the star.

- For the rest of the background, quilt swirls.

- Inside the diamonds, use a FriXion™ Gel Pen to mark points on both sides of each pieced diamond 1½" (3.81cm) and 3" (7.62cm) from the top of each pieced diamond.

- Using a machine quilting ruler, outline each pieced diamond, sew from the bottom point to the 3" (7.62cm) mark on the left, travel along the seam line to the 1½" (3.81cm) mark and sew back down to the bottom point. Continue working around the diamond in this way.

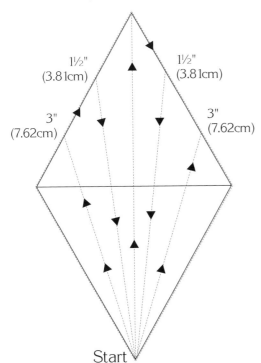

- For the colored gradated fabrics, choose one solid colored thread that matches either the lightest or darkest shade of the gradation. The thread looks different across all the shades of the gradation, blending in some spots and standing out in others.

Diamond

Finished size: 97" x 108" (246.38 x 274.32cm)

Fabric Requirements

¼ yard (22.86cm) Fabric 1

¼ yard (22.86cm) Fabric 2

⅓ yard (30.48cm) Fabric 3

⅓ yard (30.48cm) Fabric 4

½ yard (45.72cm) Fabric 5

½ yard (45.72cm) Fabric 6

½ yard (45.72cm) Fabric 7

½ yard (45.72cm) Fabric 8

½ yard (45.72cm) Fabric 9

⅓ yard (30.48cm Fabric 10

⅓ yard (30.48cm) Fabric 11

¼ yard (22.86cm) Fabric 12

¼ yard (91.45cm) Fabric 13

7¾ yards (708.66cm) Fabric 14

9 yards (822.96cm) backing and batting

Cutting

From Fabric 1, cut:
(1) 4½" (11.43cm) x WOF strip

From Fabric 2, cut:
(1) 4½" (11.43cm) x WOF strip

From Fabric 3, cut:
(2) 4½" (11.43cm) x WOF strips

From Fabric 4, cut:
(2) 4½" (11.43cm) x WOF strips

From Fabric 5, cut:
(3) 4½" (11.43cm) x WOF strips

From Fabric 6, cut:
(3) 4½" (11.43cm) x WOF strips

From Fabric 7, cut:
(3) 4½" (11.43cm) x WOF strips

From Fabric 8, cut:
(3) 4½" (11.43cm) x WOF strips

From Fabric 9, cut:
(3) 4½" (11.43cm) x WOF strips

From Fabric 10, cut:
(2) 4½" (11.43cm) x WOF strips

From Fabric 11, cut:
(2) 4½" (11.43cm) x WOF strips

From Fabric 12, cut:
(1) 4½" (11.43cm) x WOF strips

From Fabric 13, cut:
(1) 4½" (11.43cm) x WOF strips

From Fabric 14, cut:
(2) 28¾" (73.03cm) x WOF strips

(6) 5¼" (13.34cm) x WOF strips.
    From the strips, cut:
      (6) 5¼" x by 33" (13.34cm x 83.82cm) strips

(1) 97½" x 40½" (247.65 x 102.87cm) strip

(11) 2½" (6.35cm) x WOF strips for binding

Assembly Instructions

1. Using the 4½" (11.43cm) strips, cut diamonds in the following colors and numbers:
   - Fabric 1: 3 diamonds
   - Fabric 2: 6 diamonds
   - Fabric 3: 9 diamonds
   - Fabric 4: 12 diamonds
   - Fabric 5: 15 diamonds
   - Fabric 6: 18 diamonds
   - Fabric 7: 21 diamonds
   - Fabric 8: 18 diamonds
   - Fabric 9: 15 diamonds
   - Fabric 10: 12 diamonds
   - Fabric 11: 9 diamonds
   - Fabric 12: 6 diamonds
   - Fabric 13: 3 diamonds

NOTE: Refer to directions on Cutting Diamonds on page 12.

2. Sew the diamonds together into rows. You will need three of each row. Sew the diamonds together, left to right, in the following order:
   - Row 1: Fabrics 1, 2, 3, 4, 5, 6, 7
   - Row 2: Fabrics 2, 3, 4, 5, 6, 7, 8
   - Row 3: Fabrics 3, 4, 5, 6, 7, 8, 9
   - Row 4: Fabrics 4, 5, 6, 7, 8, 9, 10
   - Row 5: Fabrics 5, 6, 7, 8, 9, 10, 11
   - Row 6: Fabrics 6, 7, 8, 9, 10, 11, 12
   - Row 7: Fabrics 7, 8, 9, 10, 11, 12, 13

Refer to page 17 to cut triangles for this quilt.

Pro Tip:

In order to get perfect points when you sew the diamonds together, put a pin directly through the edge of the joining diamonds, ¼" (0.64cm) from the side of the pieces.

Hold the pieces firmly and place the pin perpendicular to the fabric. Repeat with a second pin. This will ensure your points stay in place.

3. Sew rows together to complete three large diamonds.

Cutting Large Background Triangles

Refer to page 17 to cut triangles for this quilt.

For this step, you will need to mark lines with a pencil or a FriXion™ Gel Pen. It's my favorite marking tool! The marks from it can be removed with heat if you make a mistake and need to "erase" a line. You will also need a 6" x 24" (15.24 x 60.96cm) ruler with 30° and 60° lines.

1. Prepare the two, 28¾" (73.03cm) x WOF strips from Fabric 14 by cutting off the selvages to square up the edges of each piece. Draw a ¼" (0.64cm) line from the cut edge across the width of each strip.

2. Referring to cutting instructions on page 17, and working with one strip at a time, mark the strip to create two half-equilateral triangles and one 60° triangle.

3. Repeat the step-by-step for the second fabric strip. You will cut a total of four equilateral triangles and eight half-equilateral triangles. There will be four extra equilateral triangles when you assemble the quilt top.

Assembling the Quilt Top

1. Arrange the diamonds and triangles, referring to Assembly Diagram 1.

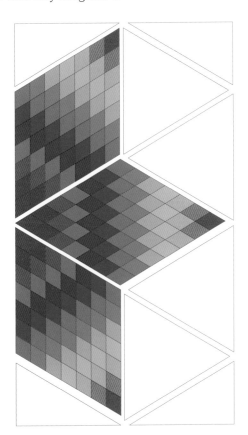

Assembly Diagram 1

2. Sew the quilt into wedges, first adding large triangles to the diamonds, then adding the half-equilateral triangles as shown in Assembly Diagram 2.

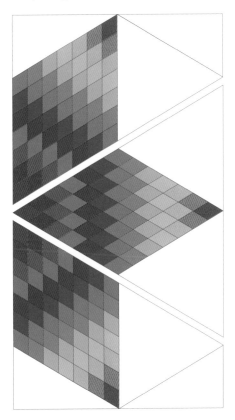

Assembly Diagram 2

3. Sew the sections together, referring to Diagram Assembly 3 to complete the star.

4. Sew the 40½" x 97½" (247.65 x 102.87cm) strip to the right side of the star.

5. Sew six, 5¼" x 33" (13.34 x 83.82cm) strips into two, 5¼" x 97½" (13.34 x 102.87cm) strips.

6. Sew the strips from step 5 to the top and bottom of the quilt center, as shown in Assembly Diagram 3.

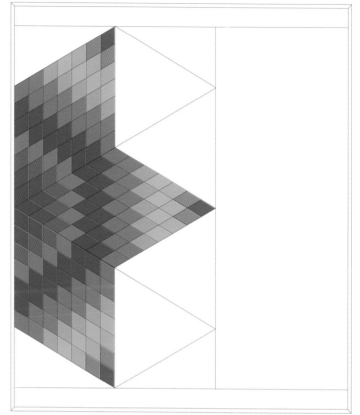

Assembly Diagram 3

Finishing the Quilt

1. Layer the quilt top, batting, and backing together. Refer to Stephanie's Quilting Designs (page 79) or quilt as desired.

2. Sew the binding strips together end-to-end to make one long binding strip. Press the seams open.

3. Press the strip wrong sides together. Sew it to the front of the quilt along the raw edges. Fold the binding over to the back, covering the raw edges and hand stitch in place.

NOTE: Refer to The Quilt Sandwich, page 20, and Continuous Binding, page 22.

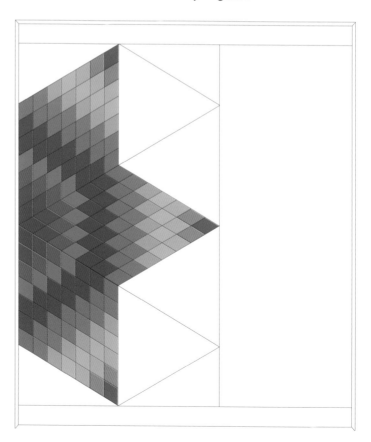

Stephanie's Quilting Designs

- This quilt has a massive amount of negative space that just begs for custom quilting. So I called in award-winning quilter Natalia Bonner to have some fun with the quilting.

- The designer of the 4-N-1 Machine Quilting Ruler that is one of my go-to quilting tools, I knew this quilt would be in good hands with Natalia. I love her style and trust her quilting instincts to help bring my pattern to life. Those two elements are necessary in creating a good relationship with your longarmer.

- Natalia used the 4-N-1 Machine Quilting Ruler to stitch-in-the-ditch along the seam lines between each diamond, and quilt arcs.

- Then she used the 4-N-1 Machine Quilting Ruler to extend the diamond with quilting. First up was a series of lines parallel to the diamond. She used the ruler to space the lines equally apart.

- The second extension is a line of feathers following the points of the diamond. These designs are echoed in the right corners of the quilt, adding balance.

- The rest of the quilt was quilted with one of Natalia's easier feather designs that combines a swirl and a feather. With minimal back stitching, this feather design requires less precision than traditional feather designs and can be used as a free motion filler.

- One nice extra element Natalia incorporated was using wool batting. The extra loft adds more dimension to the quilting, making the stitches and texture look more dramatic. Wool isn't necessary for every quilt, but when you plan on creating a quilting design you want to show off, it is a good batting choice to make.

Meet Stephanie

About the Author

Growing up, Stephanie Soebbing had one goal: to make a career out of writing. Really she just wanted to be creative, but it took some time to figure that out. She started her career as a journalist and then moved into digital marketing.

While she was pregnant with her first child, Stephanie was looking for a way out of the rat race of the advertising world so she could have more flexibility to be with her daughter.

That "way out" came when she first started teaching students her first Block of the Month design at her local quilt shop. She published her pattern online and combined her marketing, story-telling and video production training from her journalism days into her blog, *www.quiltaddictsanonymous.com*. It became a fast-growing pattern design company and fabric store.

Four years and eight block-of-the-month designs later, those first students have turned into thousands of quilters worldwide who have been inspired by Stephanie's designs and video tutorials. Today she works with her husband at their quilt shop, Quilt Addicts Anonymous, in Rock Island, Illinois. Walk into her store and you may see her daughter pulling bolts of fabric from shelves and asking for a new dress.

You can find more of Stephanie's original patterns at *http://shop.quiltaddictsanonymous.com* and browse dozens of free quilting tutorials at *quiltaddictsanonymous.com/tutorials*.

Special Thanks

Art Gallery Fabrics, Clothworks, ME+YOU and QT Fabrics for providing fabrics for the quilts in this book.

Landauer Publishing and Fox Chapel Publishing for making my dream of writing a quilt pattern book come true.

Adam Soebbing, my wonderful husband and business partner. Thank you for supporting me in so many ways, but specifically for never expecting me to make dinner every night or do the laundry, and for being an equal partner in parenting so that I can run a creative business.